THE
BOOK OF
FACTS
AND
RECORDS

THE
BOOK OF
FACTS
AND
RECORDS

Brenda and Brian Williams

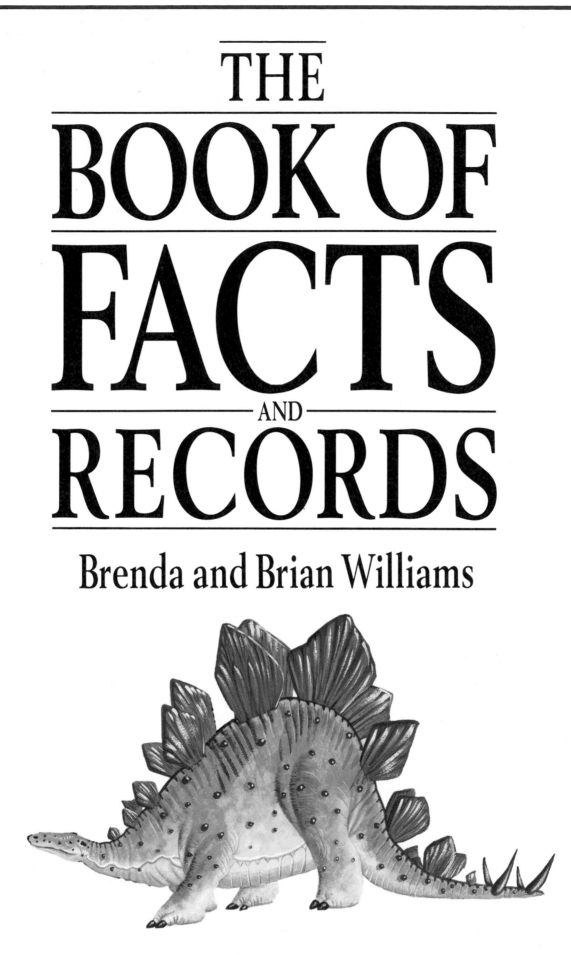

DERRYDALE BOOKS
New York

First published in 1989 by Kingfisher Books.

Copyright © Grisewood & Dempsey Ltd. 1989.

This 1990 edition published by Derrydale Books,
distributed by Crown Publishers, Inc.,
225 Park Avenue South, New York, New York 10003.

Printed and bound in Italy.

ISBN 0-517-03050-9

h g f e d c b a

Edited by John Grisewood
Assistant Editor Annabel Ramsbotham
Designed by Steve Leaning
Phototypeset by Tradespools Ltd
Printed in Italy

The publishers wish to thank the following for supplying
photographs for the book:
p. 43 All-Sport Photographic Ltd; p. 47 Decca;
p. 76 Maritshius, The Hague; p. 77 The Mansell Collection.
The publishers wish to thank the following artists for
contributing to the book:
Sue Barclay (John Martin and Artists Ltd) pp. 44/45, 50/51,
60/61, 68/69, 76/77, 80/81; Peter Bull pp. 48/49, 72–75;
Stephen Conlin pp. 54/55, 58/59; Chris Forsey pp. 22–27,
56/57, cover; David Holmes (Garden Studio) pp. 30–33,
36/37; Gillian Hurry (Linda Rogers Associates) pp. 28/29,
34/35; Ron Jobson (Jillian Burgess Artists) pp. 12–19,
46/47, 64/65, 78/79, 82–87; Kevin Maddison pp. 62/63,
66/67, 70/71; Tony Morris (Linda Rogers Associates)
pp. 38–41; Ralph Orme pp. 52/53; Martin Salisbury (Linda
Rogers Associates) pp. 20/21.

INTRODUCTION

Some facts remain true for generation after generation. For example, we know that the Earth spins around the Sun. Other facts change day by day — like the number of people living in China. However, even facts believed to be true for centuries may one day be proved wrong: before the 1500s most people thought that the Sun circled the Earth. Facts alter all the time with new knowledge. New feats and discoveries create new records.

In this book are a selection of fascinating facts and records about our world. They are grouped into eight subject areas of particular interest to inquisitive data-collectors: the universe and space, our planet, the natural world, people, places, history, science, and transportation.

Each colorful page is packed with an assortment of factual details. Some are momentous, others more trivial. All are fun and informative, highlighting the wonder and variety of the universe in which we live. Some may answer questions you have never even thought of. How far away are the stars? How big was a dinosaur's brain? Which country has the most thunderstorms? You will find these and hundreds of other amazing facts in the various chapters, which are arranged in clearly headed topics to help you find an area of special interest.

Everyone likes to know about the first, the biggest, the fastest, the oldest . . . This is a book for all to enjoy dipping into, but it is also a valuable source of reference information. The index on page 88 will help you find your way quickly to the fact or record you are seeking.

Contents

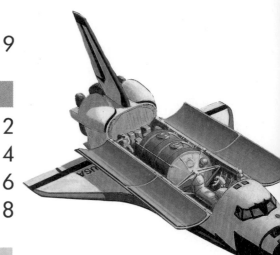

The Stars

STAR FACTS

There are so many stars in the night sky that no one can count them. There are millions and millions of galaxies ("star clusters") in the Universe, each containing many millions of stars.

The star nearest to Earth is our own Sun. The next closest is called Proxima Centauri. Light from it takes more than four years to reach us.

The most distant stars are 5 billion light-years away from Earth (about 30,000 billion billion miles). They form a new star cluster, discovered by scientists in 1988.

Stars are made of huge clouds of very hot gas. The more material they contain, the hotter and brighter they are.

spiral galaxy

OUR GALAXY IS THE MILKY WAY

The Milky Way is a spiral galaxy. From above, it looks like a spinning wheel with long "arms." Seen from the side, it looks a bit like an upturned plate. It takes about 100,000 years for light to travel across the Galaxy.

The first scientist to look into space through a telescope was Galileo Galilei of Italy. He did so in 1608. He was amazed to see spots on the Sun and craters on the Moon.

The Andromeda Galaxy is spiral-shaped, like our own. Some galaxies are egg-shaped (elliptical). Others are irregular in shape. Everything in space is moving, because the Universe is getting bigger all the time.

Big Bang

Many scientists think that the Universe started with a huge explosion more than 15 billion years ago. Scientists call this the Big Bang theory.

Some stars are much bigger than our Sun. We call them blue giants. Others, called red dwarfs, are smaller. An aging star may "balloon" to become a huge ball of thinly spread gas before shrinking and cooling to become a faint white dwarf. Finally, it "dies" and becomes a black dwarf, almost invisible.

black hole

The largest stars sometimes blow up as "supernovas." The star collapses into a tiny but amazingly heavy neutron star. Not even light can escape from its enormous gravity. The result is a "black hole."

This is where we are in our Galaxy.

shooting star

The most famous comet is named after the astronomer Edmund Halley (1656–1742). Halley's Comet was first seen in 240 B.C.

comet

The core of a comet is like a small, dirty "snowball," made of rock and ice. As it comes near to the Sun and warms up, the comet gives off a bright "tail" of gas. The tail may be millions of miles long.

A shooting star flashes across the heavens. It is a tiny lump of rock, called a meteoroid. As it hits the Earth's atmosphere, it glows white hot and burns up. A few are big enough to hit the ground. We call these, meteorites.

The Sun and Planets

The Sun is a medium-sized star. Even so, it is as big as a million Earths. On the surface it is about 10,000 degrees Fahrenheit. The center is about 25 million degrees.

Mars

Earth

Venus

Mercury

Mercury is the planet nearest the Sun and therefore the hottest. You could bake a cake on the surface of Mercury!

Venus is 67 million miles from the Sun. Mars is 142 million miles from the Sun. Our planet Earth orbits the Sun at a distance of 93 million miles. Venus is a world of deserts and mountains hidden by swirling gas clouds. Mars has mountains, craters and what look like dried-up rivers. The Martian sky is pink and the planet is always bitterly cold.

SOLAR SYSTEM FACTS

The Sun is much larger than its planets in the Solar System. If the Sun were as big as a soccer ball, the Earth would be as small as a pea.

The Sun is 93 million miles away from the Earth. It measures 865,000 miles across. That is 109 times the diameter of the Earth. It is 330,000 times heavier than the Earth.

If you could fly in a modern jet to the Sun, it would take you 19 years to get there!

Mercury, Venus, Mars, Jupiter, and Saturn can be seen with the naked eye.

Three planets (Saturn, Jupiter, and Uranus) have rings of matter circling around them.

The planet with the most moons is Saturn, with 24 — most of them are giant "snowballs" circling the planet.

NEVER LOOK DIRECTLY AT THE SUN

Jupiter

Jupiter is the biggest planet. All the other planets could be squeezed inside it. It appears to be a whirling, liquid planet made of hydrogen and other chemicals.

Saturn has more rings than any other planet. The rings form a flat band 20 times as wide as the Earth. The rings may be the remains of a shattered moon.

To measure the huge distances of space we use "light-years." Light travels amazingly fast: at 186,000 miles a second. In one year, light travels about 6,000 billion miles — we call this one light-year.

Saturn

Other star systems contain planets. In 1988 astronomers discovered a planet 30,000 times bigger than the Earth. It is 90 light years away, orbiting a "sun" known as HD114762.

Neptune   Pluto

Asteroids are miniature planets. The largest is called Ceres and is only 620 miles across.

Nicolaus Copernicus (1473–1543) was a Polish astronomer. Before Copernicus most people thought the Earth was the center of the Universe. He showed that in fact the Earth, and the other planets, orbit the Sun.

Uranus

The outer planets are the ones farthest from the Sun. Jupiter is the largest and also spins the fastest. Saturn is the second biggest planet. It is the only planet that could float in water (if there was an ocean vast enough). Next come Uranus and Neptune, both about four times as big as the Earth.

The planet farthest from the Sun is normally Pluto. But between 1979 and 1999 Pluto's orbit swings inside that of Neptune. So Neptune is at present the most distant planet.

The Moon

MOON FACTS

The Moon is about 239,000 miles away. It is 2,160 miles across — roughly as wide as Australia.

The Earth weighs 81 times as much as the Moon.

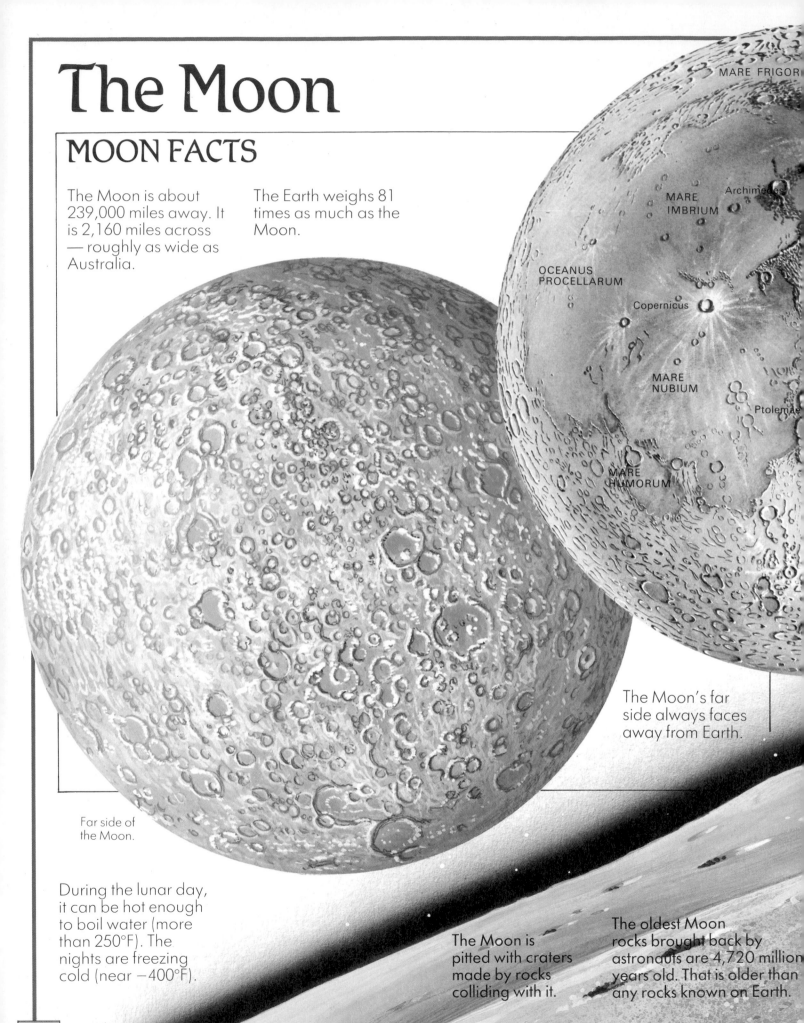

MARE FRIGOR

MARE IMBRIUM

Archimedes

OCEANUS PROCELLARUM

Copernicus

MARE NUBIUM

Ptolemae

MARE HUMORUM

The Moon's far side always faces away from Earth.

Far side of the Moon.

During the lunar day, it can be hot enough to boil water (more than 250°F). The nights are freezing cold (near −400°F).

The Moon is pitted with craters made by rocks colliding with it.

The oldest Moon rocks brought back by astronauts are 4,720 million years old. That is older than any rocks known on Earth.

16

Near side of the Moon.

Moon

Sun

Earth

MARE SERENITATIS

MARE CRISIUM

MARE IMBRIUM

MARE TRANQUILLITATIS

MARE FECUNDITATIS

MARE NECTARIS

An eclipse of the Sun happens when the Moon passes between the Earth and the Sun, cutting off the light and turning day into night for a while.

An eclipse halted a battle between the armies of ancient Lydia and Medea in 585 B.C.. The soldiers were terrified of the sudden darkness.

The first Moon landing took place on July 20, 1969. The explorers were the Apollo 11 astronauts Neil Armstrong and Edwin Aldrin.

Apollo 15

The Moon has no atmosphere. In order to breathe there, astronauts must wear spacesuits equipped with oxygen.

Lunar Rover

Gravity on the Moon is only one-sixth of that on the Earth. So an astronaut weighs less and can jump much farther than he or she could ever do on Earth.

The first vehicle to be driven on the Moon was the American lunar rover, used by the astronauts of Apollo 15 in 1971.

Space Exploration

SPACE FIRSTS

The first artificial Earth satellite was Russia's Sputnik 1 (1957). ❶

The first person to "walk" in space was Aleksei Leonov (U.S.S.R.) in 1965. A few weeks later, U.S. astronaut Edward H. White did the same, from Gemini 4. ❷

The world's first space traveler was Laika, a Russian dog (1957).

The first human space explorer was Yuri Gagarin (U.S.S.R.), on April 12, 1961.

Telstar (1962) was the first communications satellite. ❸ Today, the latest Intelsats can carry as many as 12,000 telephone calls at once. ❹

The first space station was the U.S.S.R.'s Salyut 1, launched in 1971. ❺

The Pioneer 10 probe (launched 1972) has gone beyond the orbit of Pluto and so has left the solar system. The faster-moving Voyager 1 (launched 1979) will set even greater distance records. ❼

A "step" rocket is made up of two or three stages. Each stage has its own rocket engines, which are fired in turn. The used stages fall back to Earth. ❽

The world's largest rocket is the U.S.S.R.'s Energya (1987). It weighs 2,000 tons and can lift a load of 130 tons into orbit.

Tons of space junk are orbiting the Earth. The junk includes worn-out satellites, bits of rocket booster and even a screwdriver lost by one of the astronauts!

Eating and drinking in space can be a problem. Washing has to be done inside a closed shower-bag (to stop water droplets floating all around the spacecraft).

The Earth

The Earth's atmosphere is a mixture of gases we call air.

The Earth's "skin" is a thin crust of rock. It is thinner (about 3 miles) beneath the oceans than beneath mountains (about 20 miles).

The Earth's outer core is a layer of melted metal 1,400 miles thick.

The Earth's inner core of metal measures 1,400 miles across. The Earth's center is as hot as the surface of the Sun — at least 7,000°F.

The Earth's light rocky crust floats on the mantle. As the mantle moves, the continents move too. This is "continental drift".

The mantle is a 1,700 mile thick layer of hot rock. Parts of it have a gummy consistency.

In the atmosphere, a layer of gas called ozone protects us from harmful rays from the Sun. Above the Antarctic, there is a "hole" in the ozone layer. Scientists think this is caused by the chemicals in aerosol sprays and refrigerators.

mantle

outer core

inner core

atmosphere

EARTH FACTS

The Earth weighs 6,000 quintillion tons.

The Earth's total surface area is 196,950,000 square miles.

The Earth spins around in space once every 24 hours. It takes 365¼ days to travel once around the Sun.

The Earth was "born" 4.6 billion years ago.

Around its middle, at the Equator, the Earth measures 24,900 miles.

Standing on the Earth, it is hard to believe that the planet is spinning like a giant top. At the Equator, the Earth spins at more than 1,000 mph.

The Earth is not perfectly round. It flattens at the North and South Poles and bulges at the Equator.

Arctic Ocean

North America

Atlantic Ocean

Europe

Africa

Equator

South America

Antarctica

Asia is the world's largest continent. It is twice as big as North America and four times as big as Europe.

The world's oceans run into one another to make one big watery mass.

The Equator is an imaginary line around the Earth. Most of the Earth's land lies north of the Equator.

Over 200 million years ago, the continents were joined together to form a super-continent scientists now call Pangaea. Then the continents broke apart.

On a map, lines of latitude run east-west. Lines of longitude run north-south. The Equator is latitude 0°. The North Pole is 90° North. The line of 0° longitude runs through Greenwich in London, England.

About one-tenth of the world's land is covered by ice sheets. About one-fiftieth of the world's water is always frozen.

Around the South Pole the thickest ice sheet is 16,000 feet deep. That is almost deep enough to bury Mont Blanc, the highest mountain in the European Alps.

North America

Asia

Pacific Ocean

Equator

Australia

Antarctica

21

Oceans and Rivers

If all the water in the Earth's atmosphere fell as one big shower of rain it would cover the world in water an inch deep.

The largest freshwater lake is Lake Superior in Canada. With an area of 31,759 square miles, it is almost as big as the State of Maine.

Lake Superior

Rivers meeting the sea may form vast muddy flatlands called deltas.

The world's largest river delta is in Bangladesh. It covers 29,000 square miles (bigger than West Virginia).

SEA FACTS

The sea is salty because rivers wash minerals, in particular salt, into it.

The biggest ocean is the Pacific. It covers 63,800,000 square miles.

The Atlantic, the second biggest ocean, is only half the size of the Pacific.

97%   3%

More than 97 percent of the water on Earth is in the oceans.

Pacific Ocean

71%

29%

Oceans cover 71 percent of the Earth.

The Earth's first shower of rain lasted for 60,000 years. It filled up all the oceans and seas as the Earth was being formed millions of years ago.

The oceans contain 496,370,000 cubic miles of water.

No sunlight ever reaches the ocean bottom. Below about 5,000 feet it is cold and pitch-black.

Mountains on the seabed are higher than those on land. The island of Hawaii is the tip of an undersea mountain more than 9000 metres high.

The ocean floor is slimy with mud and ooze — the remains of dead plants and animals that float down from above.

The "water cycle" keeps the world's water in circulation. Water from the oceans is drawn up as vapor by the Sun's heat. It is blown over land, cools, and falls as rain. Rivers return the water to the ocean.

The largest raindrop ever recorded fell in Hawaii in 1986. It was as big as a pea.

The longest river is the Nile in Africa, which is 4,145 miles long.

Water plunges 3,200 feet over the Angel Falls in Venezuela — the highest waterfall in the world.

The water we drink today is at least 3 billion years old — for that is when it first appeared on Earth. Since then the same water has been "recycled" over and over again.

Chalk cliffs are made from the ancient skeletons of tiny sea creatures.

The world's muddiest river is the Hwang Ho in China, also called the Yellow River. It carries enough silt to build a wall 10 feet wide and 10 feet high that would stretch 27 times around the Earth.

The *Trieste* has dived deeper than any other submarine — nearly to the bottom of the Mariana Trench.

The deepest point in the oceans is the Mariana Trench in the Pacific Ocean. It is 36,000 feet deep, and could easily swallow Mount Everest.

Sea waves are made by winds blowing on the water. The highest wave ever recorded was in 1933 when a ship survived a wave 11 feet high.

There is enough water in the oceans to provide 365 million tons for every person on Earth.

Mountains, Rocks, and Volcanoes

Lava is melted rock that spews out from an erupting volcano. Some flows like red-hot mud. Other lava is hurled out in lumps.

The highest active volcano is called Ojos de Salado. it is 22,500 feet high in the South American Andes mountains.

There are more than 600 active volcanoes. About 80 of them are under the sea.

The volcano Krakatoa in Indonesia erupted in 1883 and the sound was heard 3,000 miles away in Australia.

QUAKE FACTS

Every year there are about 1,000 earthquakes severe enough to do damage.

Earthquakes can cause undersea shocks which send huge waves, called tsunamis, surging across the ocean.

The world's worst earthquake of modern times was in China in 1976. Over 250,000 people are said to have been killed.

The first oil well was drilled in Pennsylvania, in 1859.

The world's biggest pure gold nugget was found in Australia in 1869. It gave almost 154 pounds of pure gold.

Coal is a form of carbon. Coal seams (layers) are remains of plants that grew 300 million years ago.

The largest diamond ever found was the Cullinan, discovered in South Africa in 1905. It weighed 3,106 carats.

For each one-carat (0.007 ounce) diamond, more than 250 tons of rock ore have to be mined.

Diamond is the hardest gemstone and can cut glass.

24

Mountains are formed by upward movements and folding of the Earth's rocky crust.

High mountains are "young" and still growing. Old mountains are worn away by wind, rain, and ice.

The oldest rocks found on land are 4.3 billion years old. The oldest rocks found beneath the oceans are only 200 million years old.

The highest mountain on Earth is Mount Everest in the Himalayas. Its peak is 29,028 feet above sea level.

Mountaineering as a sport began in the 1850s.

Grand Canyon

Old Faithful, a geyser (hot spring) in Yellowstone National Park, erupts for five minutes every hour.

The longest river gorge in the world is the Grand Canyon in Arizona, which is approximately 217 miles long.

A fossil is the hardened remains of a dead plant or animal. Fossils form when mud and sand harden into rock.

The largest cave system is in Kentucky. It extends for over 330 miles.

The Réseau Jean Bernard cave in France is the deepest, at 5,036 feet.

Caves are hollowed out of soft rock by underground streams.

Stalactites hang downward inside caves. They form when slow-dripping mineral deposits harden.

In the same way, stalagmites grow like pillars from the floor of a cave.

Deserts and Forests

CONIFEROUS FOREST

The larch and swamp cypress are coniferous trees that shed their leaves. All the other conifers are evergreen.

Snow slides off the sloping branches of conifers in winter.

Coniferous (cone-bearing) trees grow in the colder regions of the Earth.

North America

Forests cover about 25 percent of the land.

DECIDUOUS FOREST

Much of northern Europe was once covered in deciduous forest.

During a great storm in 1987, 15 million trees in southern England were blown down.

Broad-leaved or deciduous trees shed their leaves in autumn.

Trees act as the Earth's "lungs." They take in nitrogen and release oxygen into the air.

RAIN FOREST

Rain forest grows in hot, wet regions near the Equator.

The world's largest rain forest is the Amazon forest of South America.

There are more than 3,000 species of trees in the rain forests of Indonesia alone.

Trees in the rain forest grow to about 150 feet high.

When rain forest is cut down, the soil soon loses its richness, leaving scrub and desert.

South America

In 1988 an area of Amazon rain forest as big as West Germany was cut down. The forest is being destroyed to raise cattle for beef.

The world's tallest trees are the giant redwoods of California, which grow to more than 360 feet high.

COLD DESERTS

The biggest iceberg was 11,000 square miles — larger than the state of Maryland. Icebergs break off from the ends of glaciers when they reach the sea.

Glaciers are slow-moving "rivers" of ice. The longest glacier is the Lambert in the Antarctic (more than 250 miles long).

Some glaciers "sprint" 400 feet in one day, and then stop for years. The world's fastest glacier is in Greenland and moves about 78 feet every day.

Europe

Hot deserts cover about 20 percent of the land.

Africa

HOT DESERTS

The world's biggest desert is the Sahara in Africa. At 3½ million square miles, it is 16 times the size of France.

The Sahara was once fertile. Rivers flowed across it and trees grew there.

Only about 20 per-cent of the Sahara is soft sand. The rest is stone and pebbles.

The driest place on Earth is the Atacama Desert in Chile. Until 1971 no rain had fallen there for 400 years.

An oasis is a waterhole in the desert. The water comes from an underground lake or stream.

Most desert dwellers are nomads, wandering in search of water and food for their animals.

Sand dunes can be as high as 1,300 feet.

Sand dunes move. Like waves in the ocean, they are blown across the desert.

The polar regions of the Arctic and the Antarctic are the largest cold deserts.

The Antarctic was once a warm continent, with trees and plants.

Antarctica

27

Weather and Climate

COLD FACTS

Snowflakes are all six-sided crystals of frozen water vapor, but no two flakes have the same pattern.

Most of North America and Europe were covered by ice 10,000 years ago, during the last Ice Age.

The coldest place on Earth is the Antarctic, where temperatures are as low as —128°F.

Rainbows appear when sunlight passes through water drops in the sky.

The world's heaviest hailstones were reported in 1986, in Bangladesh. They weighed more than 2 pounds each, (six times as heavy as a baseball).

Clouds are formed by water vapor rising into the sky, where it cools to become water droplets.

"Weather" exists only in the troposphere — the lowest zone of the Earth's atmosphere — about 10 miles above the Earth's surface.

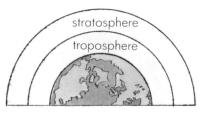

stratosphere

troposphere

The seasons change as the Earth moves around the Sun. Different parts of the Earth have more sunlight, and heat, at different times of the year.

WET AND WINDY FACTS

We measure the speed of winds on the Beaufort scale, named after a British admiral.

There are a million microscopic water droplets in a single raindrop.

The Chinese were the first people to use umbrellas, around 3,000 years ago.

A gentle breeze blowing at 7—12 mph is Force 3. A gale howling at 40—46 mph is Force 8.

Cherrapunji in India holds the record for most rain in a month (366 inches) and in a year (1,041 inches).

Winds blow because of differences in air pressure and temperature. Air flows from high pressure regions to low pressure regions.

HOT FACTS

The hottest place on Earth is in Libya, North Africa. In 1922 the temperature reached 136°F.

The Italian Galileo Galilei was the first scientist to measure temperature with a thermometer, in 1607.

A warm water current called the North Atlantic Drift keeps winters in Britain milder than in mainland Europe.

By burning coal, oil, gasoline, and natural gas as fuel in our homes, factories, and cars we could be making the world warmer. By the year 2050 the Earth may be up to four degrees warmer than it is now.

At the North and South Poles, in summer there may be up to 147 days of "midnight sun" when the sun never sets fully.

Each raindrop splits up white sunlight into different colors of the spectrum.

The Sahara has only 80 daylight hours without sunshine in a year.

Each year, there are as many as 16 million thunderstorms. Bogor in Java has had 322 thundery days in a year.

Thunder is caused by the tremendous expansion of the air heated as a lightning flash passes through it.

STORMY FACTS

Hurricanes form over warm sea, sucking up air into a whirling funnel of cloud. The clouds in a hurricane spiral up to 60 miles long and rise 66,000 feet high.

Hurricane winds whirl faster and faster, yet within the center or "eye" of the storm the air is calm.

Hurricanes in the Far East and the western Pacific are called typhoons. In the Indian Ocean they are called cyclones.

A tornado can whip across country at up to 30 mph. Its name means "twister." The winds at the outer edge of a tornado spin at more than 400 mph.

A lightning flash heats the air around it to three times the temperature of the Sun.

Count the seconds between a lightning flash and the sound of its thunder. Divide the figure by five to find how many miles away the storm is.

Hunters and Hunted

A baby wildebeest can run within minutes of being born.

Grazing animals of the African plains migrate every year to find fresh pasture. Wildebeest can detect a rain shower 30 miles away.

The zebra's stripes help to confuse a hunter, such as a lion. As the zebras gallop away in a group, the lion finds it more difficult to pick out a single victim.

Tick birds "clean" rhinos by eating insect parasites that live on their skin.

NATURAL FACTS

Over one million animal species are alive today. More than 950,000 of these species are insects. Only 4,500 are mammals.

Countless millions of animals once roamed Africa's plains. But since 1900, Africa's wildlife has shrunk by 70 percent. In the last 300 years 300 of the world's animal species have died out.

The extinct Cape and Barbary lions were the biggest African lions, with the largest manes.

In the rain forests of South America live more than 40 species of parrot, 300 kinds of hummingbirds, and thousands of different butterflies.

The vulture's sharp eyes give it a panoramic view of the plains, plus a telescopic "close-up" to pinpoint a dead animal below.

Antelopes live in herds. With so many sharp eyes and keen noses on guard, it is not easy for an enemy to approach unnoticed.

Female lions do most of the hunting for the group, or pride. They hide in long grass, creeping forward until close enough to charge and drag down their prey.

The rhinoceros is the second largest land animal after the elephant. Two kinds of rhinoceros live in Africa: the black and the white. Both are now very rare as rhinos are killed for their horns.

The largest bird in the world is the ostrich, which stands up to 9 feet tall. It cannot fly, but it can run as fast as a galloping horse.

31

Prehistoric Life

FACTS

The first mammals were small shrew-like creatures.

The first amphibians crawled out of the water to live on dry land 300 million years ago.

The age of dinosaurs began about 225 million years ago. About 65 million years ago dinosaurs died out. No one knows why.

The fiercest of all the dinosaurs was the meat-eating **Tyrannosaurus Rex** "king of the tyrant lizards." It was almost 20 feet tall and its jaws were longer than a human!

Tyrannosaurus Rex

Prehistoric dragonflies were as big as pigeons.

baluchitherium

All these animals are drawn to scale. They did not all live at the same time.

Most dinosaurs had tiny brains. **Stegosaurus** weighed nearly two tons. But its brain was no bigger than a plum.

smilodon

stegosaurus

The saber-tooth cat **Smilodon** had long stabbing teeth. It used them to attack thick-skinned prey.

Baluchitherium was the largest land mammal of all time. It stood more than 23 feet tall.

Stegosaurus was an armored dinosaur. Its bony plates and scales protected it from the teeth of enemies.

The **moa** was an enormous flightless bird of New Zealand, twice as tall as a person. It died out only 150 years ago.

The biggest flying reptile (or **Pterosaur**) that ever lived was named **Quetzalcoatlus** by scientists. Fossil remains show it had a wingspan of 36 feet.

diplodocus

pterosaur

The enormous reptile **Diplodocus** could easily have peered over a house! But there were even larger reptiles. The earth-shaking **Seismosaurus** measured 115 feet from nose to tail and weighed twice as much as Diplodocus — 100 tons, or as much as 20 elephants.

mammoth

megatherium

killer kangaroo

Until 50,000 years ago a **killer kangaroo** hunted in Australia's rain forests. Its jagged teeth show it was a meat-eater.

Mammoths were bigger than elephants. During the Ice Age people hunted them for food.

Mammoths died out 20,000 years ago. Preserved and frozen carcasses of mammoths have been found. Their meat was still good enough to eat.

Modern sloths hang from tree branches. **Megatherium** was a giant sloth of South America. It lived on the ground.

Plant World

Like animals, plants are grouped into families. The largest family has plants with flowers and enclosed seeds — the angiosperms.

Out of 375,000 known plant species, more than 250,000 are flowering plants.

To defend themselves, plants may have thorns, spines, or poisons. One conifer tree makes a chemical to halt the growth of caterpillars that try to eat its leaves.

The desert plant called welwitschia grows only two leaves, even though it can live for 100 years.

Plants send down roots to find water. The African wild fig has roots more than 100 yards long.

foxglove

welwitschia

Many drugs come from plants. From the foxglove we get the drug digitalis, for treating heart disease.

The largest flowers belong to the rafflesia of Southeast Asia. They measure a yard across. This flower smells like decaying meat — and attracts lots of insects.

PLANT FACTS

Unhappy plants cry for help. As a thirsty plant sucks in the last drop of moisture from its fibers, it makes a high-pitched sound — too high for us to hear.

The smallest plants are a type of water-living plankton called Coccolithophoridae. Five hundred would rest on a pin head.

Among living things, only plants can make their own food. Green plants use the energy from sunlight to turn water (from the soil) and carbon dioxide gas (from the air) into glucose food.

bamboo

The world's oldest tree is the bristlecone pine. One in Arizona, started life 4,600 years ago — when the Great Pyramid of Egypt was being built.

Bamboo is the tallest and fastest-growing grass. It can grow to 100 feet at a rate of almost one yard a day.

Some plants catch insects for food. Different species use hinged leaves, funnels, sticky hairs, or trap doors to catch their prey.

Venus fly trap

sundew

rafflesia

The coco de mer palm of the Seychelles Islands has the biggest seed. Each nut weighs up to 40 pounds.

The plant with the tiniest flower is the Brazilian duckweed or wolfia. The flower measures two-hundredths of an inch across.

The giant kelp of the Pacific grows longer than any other seaweed: up to 200 feet.

wolfia

giant kelp

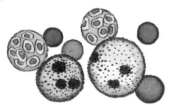

The first plants were algae that appeared on Earth more than 3 billion years ago. Flowering plants are modern. They first appeared 150 million years ago.

Fossils of the gingko or maidenhair tree (which still grows in Asia) show that it lived 200 million years ago.

In the 1600s, when tulips first reached Europe from Turkey, some people were so anxious to own them that they sold their homes to buy bulbs.

tulips

Land Animals

The biggest snake is the South American anaconda. It can grow 26 feet long and weigh 140 pounds.

African elephants have larger ears and longer tusks than Asian elephants.
The African elephant eats nearly 800 pounds of food a day. Each meal takes $2\frac{1}{2}$ days to pass through its stomach.

The kangaroo can jump four times its own length. The animal long-jump champion is the flea. It can leap 100 times its own length.

flea

The elephant's trunk is its nose, a siphon for sucking up water, and a sensitive tool for grasping food

The cheetah sprints faster than any other animal on four legs. A hunting cheetah races at almost 60 mph — but cannot keep it up for long.

BIGGEST, SMALLEST, LONGEST

The smallest land mammal is the African pygmy shrew. Only $2\frac{1}{2}$ inches long including its tail, it is one-fortieth the weight of a Goliath beetle.

The heaviest insect is the Goliath beetle of Africa, which weighs up to $3\frac{1}{2}$ ounces. It dwarfs the common ladybug.

A worm caught by a blackbird in Britain in 1988 was 6 feet long.
Worms almost 23 feet long live in southern Africa!

The giraffe is taller than any other animal. Yet its long neck has the same number of bones (seven) as yours.

Soviet scientists brought back to life a deep-frozen salamander. Trapped in ice when hibernating, it had been frozen for 90 years.

Sloths hang upside-down and sleep for 18 hours a day. A sloth leaves the trees only once a week — to visit its special "toilet."

The Goliath spider of Guyana is the world's biggest spider. It can measure up to 10 inches across and hunts birds and lizards.

Tortoises live longer than humans — up to 150 years.

BEAR FACTS

Polar bear fur looks white, but each hair is hollow and colorless. The fur traps light and heat from the sun to keep the bear warm.

Giant pandas look like bears, but belong to a separate family.

Undersea Life

A full-grown bull (male) elephant seal weighs more than three tons.

The Portuguese man of war is a jellyfish with stinging tentacles 30 feet long. The most poisonous jellyfish is the Australian sea wasp.

Flying fish glide for up to 400 feet, using their stiff fins as wings. They reach takeoff speed at around 40 mph under water.

The blue whale is the largest animal on Earth. It weighs as much as 100 tons and may be 110 feet long.

Every day a blue whale eats four tons of food. It feeds on krill (tiny shrimp-like animals).

The giant squid is a relative of the garden snail. This deepsea monster is the largest of all mollusks, up to 65 feet long.

Squids and octopuses squirt out clouds of ink to confuse an enemy.

At up to 20 feet long, the great white shark is the biggest and fiercest man-eating shark.

The blue spotted octopus is so poisonous that its bite can kill a person.

No human swimmer can match the sprinters of the ocean. Fastest are the marlin (50 mph) and tuna (45 mph). The killer whale is the fastest whale, followed by the dolphin.

Dolphin (28 mph)

Killer Whale (34 mph)

Human (3 mph)

Barracuda (20 mph)

The manta ray or devilfish has a wingspan of up to 23 feet. It is the largest of the rays.

Some sea snakes are very poisonous. A sea snake needs to surface to breathe air.

WATERY WONDERS

Seahorse

The seahorse is a devoted parent. The male carries the babies in a pouch.

The electric eel of South America can give an electric shock of 500 volts.

The Galapagos iguana is the only true marine lizard. It dives and swims, but must surface to breathe air.

Iguana

The porcupine fish is covered in prickles. If attacked, it sucks in water and air to blow itself up like a spiny balloon.

The mantis shrimp is the boxing champion of the ocean. It has an extending claw, with which it can punch a hole through a glass jar.

In the pitch-black ocean depths lurk strange creatures such as the deepsea angler. It waves a luminous lure to entice victims within range of its gaping jaws.

The archer fish spits out a jet of water to shoot down insects from overhanging leaves.

The mudskipper is a fish that ventures out of water.

Mudskipper

39

Flying Animals

peregrine falcon

Bats are the only true flying mammals. They hunt by "echo-location." The bat's high-pitched squeaks bounce back from whatever they hit — a moth, for instance. The bat's keen ears pick up the echoes, and it homes in on its prey.

bat

condor

In a dive, the peregrine falcon may exceed 180 mph.

The South American condor, a vulture, is the largest bird of prey. Its wings span 10 feet.

The world's smallest bird, the Cuban bee hummingbird, weighs less than a tenth of an ounce. It would take more than 5,000 bee hummingbirds to balance one condor on a pair of scales!

hummingbird

The cuckoo lays its egg in the nest of another bird. The cuckoo chick grows quickly and pushes out its nest-mates.

cuckoo

INSECT FACTS

An Australian dragonfly can fly at up to 30 mph.

The New Guinea Queen Alexandra's birdwing, largest of the butterflies, measures 11 inches across.

The "dance" of a honey bee tells other worker bees where to find pollen-rich flowers.

Moths have amazingly good senses of smell. A male moth can smell a female up to 7 miles away.

Grasshoppers have ears in their legs. Houseflies taste their food by stamping in it.

The Arctic tern migrates farther than any other bird. It flies from the North to the South Pole, a distance of 11,000 miles.

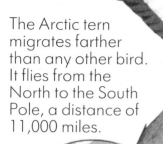

The wandering albatross has the longest wings of any bird, up to 11 feet across. These birds glide over the ocean, coming to land only to breed.

albatross

Arctic tern

When the skimmer goes fishing it flies low, trailing the bottom of its bill in the water to scoop up fish.

spine-tailed swift

In level flight, the spine-tailed swift is the speediest of all fliers: it reaches 105 mph.

skimmer

parrot

crow

weaver bird

Parrots, cockatoos, crows, and cranes live more than 70 years in zoos.

One of the most skillful nest builders is the African weaver bird.

BIRD FACTS

There are 9,000 species of birds.

During World War I, a French carrier pigeon was awarded a medal for bravery.

The ostrich lays the largest egg of any bird. You would need two dozen hen's eggs to make an ostrich-egg-sized omelette.

Archaeopteryx was a prehistoric bird-lizard. This oldest-known ancestor of modern birds lived more than 137 million years ago.

41

The Human Body

During an average lifetime a person breathes 500 million times. The heart beats about 3 billion times in a lifetime.

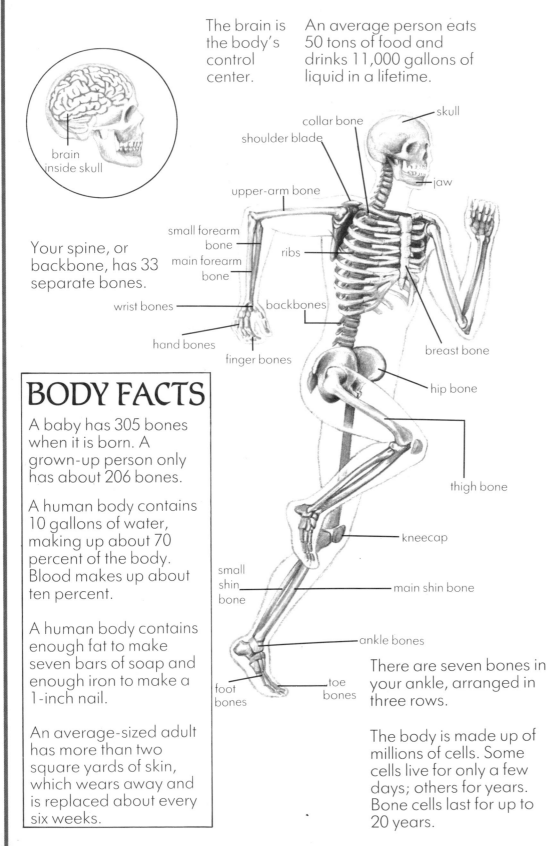

The brain is the body's control center.

brain inside skull

An average person eats 50 tons of food and drinks 11,000 gallons of liquid in a lifetime.

Your spine, or backbone, has 33 separate bones.

collar bone
shoulder blade
skull
jaw
upper-arm bone
small forearm bone
main forearm bone
ribs
wrist bones
backbones
hand bones
finger bones
breast bone
hip bone
thigh bone
kneecap
small shin bone
main shin bone
ankle bones
foot bones
toe bones

BODY FACTS

A baby has 305 bones when it is born. A grown-up person only has about 206 bones.

A human body contains 10 gallons of water, making up about 70 percent of the body. Blood makes up about ten percent.

A human body contains enough fat to make seven bars of soap and enough iron to make a 1-inch nail.

An average-sized adult has more than two square yards of skin, which wears away and is replaced about every six weeks.

There are seven bones in your ankle, arranged in three rows.

The body is made up of millions of cells. Some cells live for only a few days; others for years. Bone cells last for up to 20 years.

RECORD BODIES

The world's tallest person was an American named Robert Wadlow (1918–40). He stood 9 feet tall.

The world's most famous midget was the showman General Tom Thumb (Charles S. Stratton, 1838–83). He was 3 feet tall. A number of people even smaller have been known.

The world's smallest people are the pygmies of West Africa. Africa also has some of the tallest people, such as the Tutsi and Dinka tribes.

Jon Brower Minnoch (1941–83), an American, is believed to have weighed over 1,300 pounds. Like most overweight people, his size was caused by illness.

No human being has been proved to have lived longer than Shigechiyo Izumi of Japan. He was 120 years and 237 days old when he died in 1986.

When you walk, you use more than 200 different muscles.

There are about 10,000 taste buds in the human tongue.

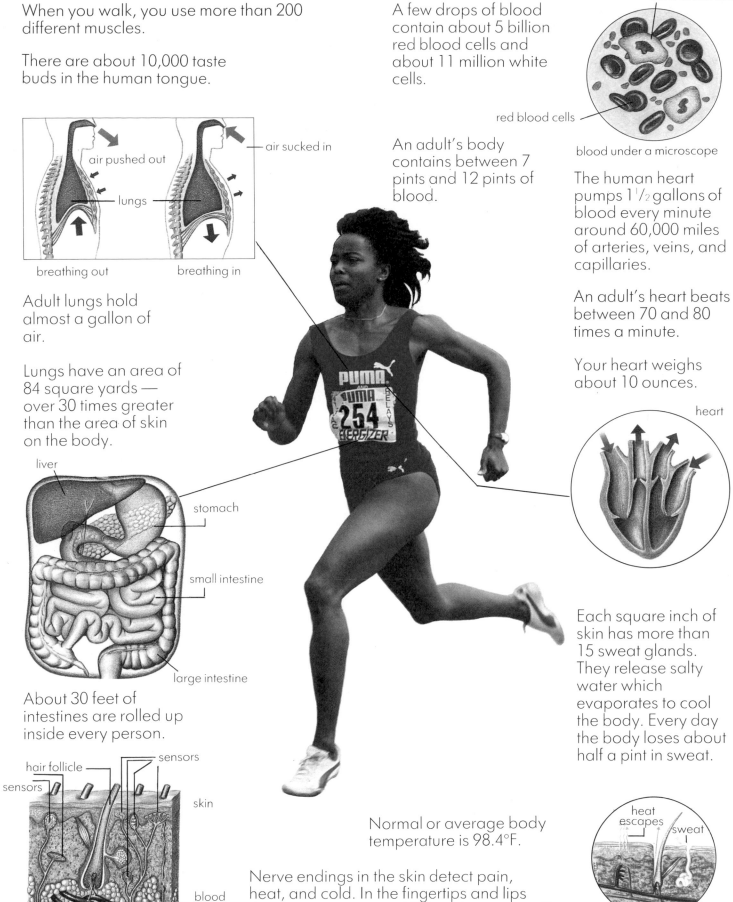

air pushed out

lungs

air sucked in

breathing out

breathing in

Adult lungs hold almost a gallon of air.

Lungs have an area of 84 square yards — over 30 times greater than the area of skin on the body.

liver

stomach

small intestine

large intestine

About 30 feet of intestines are rolled up inside every person.

sensors

hair follicle

sensors

skin

blood vessels

A few drops of blood contain about 5 billion red blood cells and about 11 million white cells.

An adult's body contains between 7 pints and 12 pints of blood.

white blood cells

red blood cells

blood under a microscope

The human heart pumps 1 1/2 gallons of blood every minute around 60,000 miles of arteries, veins, and capillaries.

An adult's heart beats between 70 and 80 times a minute.

Your heart weighs about 10 ounces.

heart

Each square inch of skin has more than 15 sweat glands. They release salty water which evaporates to cool the body. Every day the body loses about half a pint in sweat.

Normal or average body temperature is 98.4°F.

Nerve endings in the skin detect pain, heat, and cold. In the fingertips and lips there are as many as 30 "touch receptors" per square inch.

heat escapes

sweat

PUMA
PUMA
254
ENERGIZER

43

Food and Drink

To keep healthy, an adult needs 3,000 calories of food energy a day.

The United States holds half of the world's grain reserves and provides 70 percent of the cereals sent as aid to the hungry in poor countries.

Italy makes more wine than any other country.

Meat, fish, milk, vegetables, and fruit give us proteins, fats, vitamins, and minerals.

Western Europe is the largest producer of dairy foods (milk, butter, and cheese) — one-fourth of the world's total.

Factory Foods

Pasteurized milk is heated to kill germs and stop it from going bad.

Nicolas Appert won a prize from the French emperor Napoleon in 1810 for discovering how to preserve food by bottling and boiling it.

Food preserved in cans was first used in 1812 on board ship.

tea picking

FOOD FACTS

Doughnuts were invented by an American schoolboy. He asked his mother to cut out the middles of her stodgy cakes and fry them.

Spanish adventurers brought potatoes from South America to Europe in the 1500s. At first they were eaten only at rich banquets.

Oranges are the world's most popular fruit. Next come apples and pears.

Sandwiches get their name from the Earl of Sandwich (1718–92), a keen gambler who ate cold meat between two slices of bread while at the card table. Roman soldiers may have enjoyed them for their lunch, too.

An ice cream dessert, was named after Australian singer Dame Nellie Melba (1861–1931).

Peach Melba was created by a chef at London's Savoy Hotel especially for her.

Rice is the main cereal crop in hot countries where wheat cannot be grown. Rice seedlings are planted in flooded paddy fields.

rice planting

Breakfast cereals were invented in the 1800s as health foods.

An artificial "meat" food appeared in 1972. It was made from vegetable protein spun into fibers.

Tea is made from the dried leaf tips of a bush grown mainly in Asia and Africa.

Coffee is made from beans found inside berries on a tree which comes from South and Central America and Africa.

coffee picking

Chocolate and cocoa come from the tropical cacao tree.

In Europe, the tomato was grown as an ornamental plant and not eaten until the 1830s.

The Romans ate raw cabbage leaves to stop headaches.

In the 1700s Captain James Cook took cakes of "portable soup" on his long voyages. The soup was made from boiled meat and bones and looked like solid glue. But it helped keep the sailors healthy.

All parts of the coconut palm have their uses. Inside the nuts are "milk" and white "meat." The tree's trunk is used for timber, the leaf ribs make rafters for huts, and the leaf fibers can be woven into baskets, mats, and hats.

Unusual Foods

In Tibet, "tea soup" is made from tea leaves pressed into brick shapes. Bits of brick are boiled with flour dumplings and butter, and eaten with a spoon.

Bird's nest soup is made from the nests of cave-dwelling swiftlets which live in Southeast Asia. It is a Chinese delicacy.

A purple seaweed called laver is eaten in Wales. It is made into laver bread.

The Arts

The Bible is the most widely distributed book in the world. It has been translated into 303 languages.

The Russian Vaslav Nijinsky (1890–1950) was perhaps the greatest male ballet dancer of all time. He and the ballerina Anna Pavlova (1881–1931) danced for Diaghilev's Russian Ballet.

The first architect to design modern skyscrapers was Louis H. Sullivan (1856–1924).

The Taj Mahal in India was built as a tomb for the wife of Shah Jahan. Twenty thousand men worked on it from 1632 to 1650. Shah Jahan was buried there too, in 1666.

The largest library in the world is the United States Library of Congress. It contains more than 86 million items and 530 miles of shelves.

One of the world's greatest playwrights was William Shakespeare (1564–1616). The longest of his 37 plays is *Hamlet*, with 4,042 lines.

Taj Mahal

Shakespeare

It took the sculptor Michelangelo four years to paint the ceiling of the Sistine Chapel in Rome, beginning in 1508. He had to lie on scaffolding almost 100 feet above the floor. The painting covered over 10,000 square feet and in all Michelangelo painted 343 figures.

Michelangelo

The earliest paintings date from prehistoric times, perhaps as far back as 350,000 years.

The famous cave paintings at Lascaux in France, discovered in 1940, are about 20,000 years old.

Mozart Bach

Brahms Stravinsky

The largest orchestra ever was conducted in 1872 at Boston, by Johann Strauss the younger (1823–99). It had 987 instruments (including 400 first violins) and a choir of 20,000.

These four famous composers are Johann Sebastian Bach (1685–1750), Wolfgang Amadeus Mozart (1756–91), Johannes Brahms (1833–97) and Igor Stravinsky (1882–1971).

A clay "army" of over 8,000 life-size figures was discovered in 1974. The army guarded the tomb of Shih Huang Ti, first emperor of China (221–207 B.C.). No two figures are the same.

didgeridoo

The Aborigines of Australia play a wind instrument called a didgeridoo. Most are 5 foot long, but some special decorated ones are 14 feet. They are made from bamboo or hollowed-out tree trunks.

Dresden china

The world's most famous and valuable painting is thought to be the "Mona Lisa" (La Gioconda) by Leonardo da Vinci. It hangs in the Louvre Museum, in Paris.

One of the most famous artists of modern times was the Spaniard Pablo Picasso (1881–1973).

Modern artists have made sculptures from old tires, bricks, and scrap metal. A blank canvas has been described as art. So has a vast curtain hung across the Grand Canyon!

Tempera is a paint made from egg yolk mixed with dry powder color and water.

Fine porcelain, or "Dresden china," has been made at Meissen (East Germany) since the 1700s. The secret of making white porcelain was discovered by an alchemist trying to make gold.

Sports and Pastimes

OLYMPIC FACTS

The symbol of the Olympic movement is five rings linked together. The five colors (blue, yellow, black, green, and red) represent the five continents.

The Olympic Games were revived in 1896 at Athens in Greece. They have been held every four years since, except during the two world wars.

The Greek Olympic Games were held every four years from 776 B.C. until A.D. 393. But competitive Games had been held long before.

Juan Fangio (Argentina) was world motor racing champion a record five times. He was 46 when he won his last title in 1957.

The fastest human sprinter can run at just over 25 mph. A racehorse can gallop at over 40 mph.

Ice hockey is the fastest of all team games. The fastest ball game is pelota, in which the ball travels at over 180 mph.

SPORTY FACTS

The game of nine pins (skittles) was banned in some states of America in the early 1800s. So ten-pin bowling was invented instead.

The first person to windsurf across the Atlantic Ocean was Frenchman Stephane Peyron in 1987.

The longest baseball game was in 1920. Boston and Brooklyn played 26 innings, until it got dark. The score was 1-1.

On May 6, 1954 Roger Bannister ran a mile in 3 min. 59.4 sec. He was the first athlete to run a mile in under four minutes. In 1985 Steve Cram lowered the world mile record to 3 min. 46.32 sec. In a race at this speed, Cram would have finished 280 feet ahead of Bannister.

Jesse Owens (U.S.A.) set a long jump record in 1935 that remained unbroken until 1968. Bob Beamon (U.S.A.) then leapt 29 feet. He is still unbeaten.

Glass fiber poles for vaulting were first used in 1960. Before then bamboo poles were used.

The world's largest sports stadium is in Prague, Czechoslovakia, and can hold 240,000 spectators.

The Marathon race is named after a battle fought between Greeks and Persians in 490 B.C. A Greek named Pheidippides is supposed to have run 23 miles to give news of the Greek victory, dropping dead when he had delivered his message.

The Olympic torch is lit by the rays of the sun at Olympia in Greece, and carried by relays of runners to wherever the Games are being held.

At the 1972 Munich Olympics Mark Spitz (U.S.A.) won a record seven gold medals in swimming events.

Golf must have been played in the Middle Ages, for in 1457 the Scottish Parliament passed a law banning the game.

In 1873 a rule book for a game called "sphairistike" was published in England. By 1875 the game was called lawn tennis.

In the early 1300s King Edward the Second of England banned the games of soccer and bowls, because he thought people were spending too little time practicing archery.

The World Cup (for soccer) was first played for in 1930. When Brazil won for the third time, in 1970, they were awarded the Jules Rimet Trophy.

The youngest tennis player to win the Wimbledon men's singles title is Boris Becker (1985), at 17 years and 228 days. Lottie Dod won the women's championship in 1887 when aged only 15 years and 285 days.

The first person to swim the English Channel was Captain Matthew Webb in 1875.

The first recorded game of football was played between the university teams of Rutgers and Princeton in 1869.

49

Entertainment

The Great Wallendas became a world-famous circus act, forming human pyramids on a bicycle balanced on a wire 40 feet above the ring.

The first lion-tamer to put his head into a lion's mouth was the 18th-century American menagerie-owner Isaac Van Amburgh.

The world's oldest theaters are the open-air amphitheaters of Greece, such as that at Epidaurus. Plays were performed in these theaters as long ago as the fifth century B.C. The audience sat in tiers forming a near-circle around the area where the actors performed.

RADIO AND T.V.

In 1901 Guglielmo Marconi sent the first radio signals across the Atlantic Ocean.

Public radio broadcasts began in the U.S.A. in 1920. Television broadcasting was begun in 1936 by the British Broadcasting Corporation (B.B.C.).

The world's first communications satellite was Telstar (1962). For the first time live TV programs could be beamed between continents.

Television was demonstrated as early as 1924 by John Logie Baird. But eventually a different, electronic, system was chosen for worldwide use and introduced in the 1930s.

Some television sets are so small that they can be worn on the wrist like a watch.

The first films for public entertainment were shown in 1894 in Paris and New York.

The world's largest movie screen is in Jakarta, Indonesia. The biggest movie theater is in Detroit. It seats over 5,000 people.

Mickey Mouse starred in Walt Disney's first cartoon film with sound, *Steamboat Willie* (1928).

China has more movie-goers than any other country.

An 8,000-seat theater in Perth, Australia, is the world's biggest.

The world's longest-running play is Agatha Christie's thriller *The Mousetrap*. It opened in London in 1952.

MUSIC

Stereo sound experiments were made as early as the 1880s. The stereo disc was invented in 1930.

A compact disc player has a laser beam which is reflected off tiny pits in the disc's surface.

The biggest-selling record ever is Irving Berlin's *White Christmas* recorded in 1942 by singer Bing Crosby. It has sold over 170 million copies.

Stereo tape recorders playing cassettes were first sold in the 1960s.

The first pop music charts appeared in 1940 when the U.S. Billboard listings began.

The Beatles are thought to have sold more than a billion records. They were awarded 47 gold discs — a gold disc equals a million sales of a record.

Countries

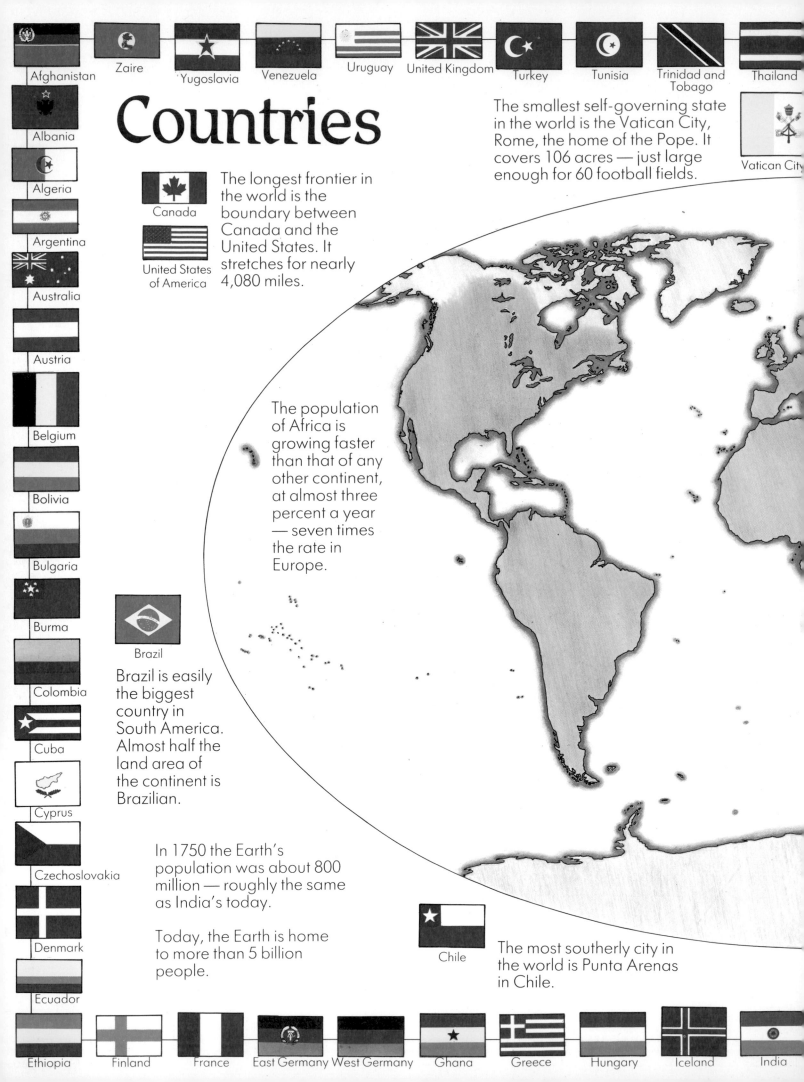

Afghanistan

Zaire

Yugoslavia

Venezuela

Uruguay

United Kingdom

Turkey

Tunisia

Trinidad and Tobago

Thailand

Albania

Algeria

Argentina

Australia

Austria

Belgium

Bolivia

Bulgaria

Burma

Colombia

Cuba

Cyprus

Czechoslovakia

Denmark

Ecuador

Vatican City

Canada

United States of America

Brazil

Chile

The smallest self-governing state in the world is the Vatican City, Rome, the home of the Pope. It covers 106 acres — just large enough for 60 football fields.

The longest frontier in the world is the boundary between Canada and the United States. It stretches for nearly 4,080 miles.

The population of Africa is growing faster than that of any other continent, at almost three percent a year — seven times the rate in Europe.

Brazil is easily the biggest country in South America. Almost half the land area of the continent is Brazilian.

In 1750 the Earth's population was about 800 million — roughly the same as India's today.

Today, the Earth is home to more than 5 billion people.

The most southerly city in the world is Punta Arenas in Chile.

Ethiopia

Finland

France

East Germany

West Germany

Ghana

Greece

Hungary

Iceland

India

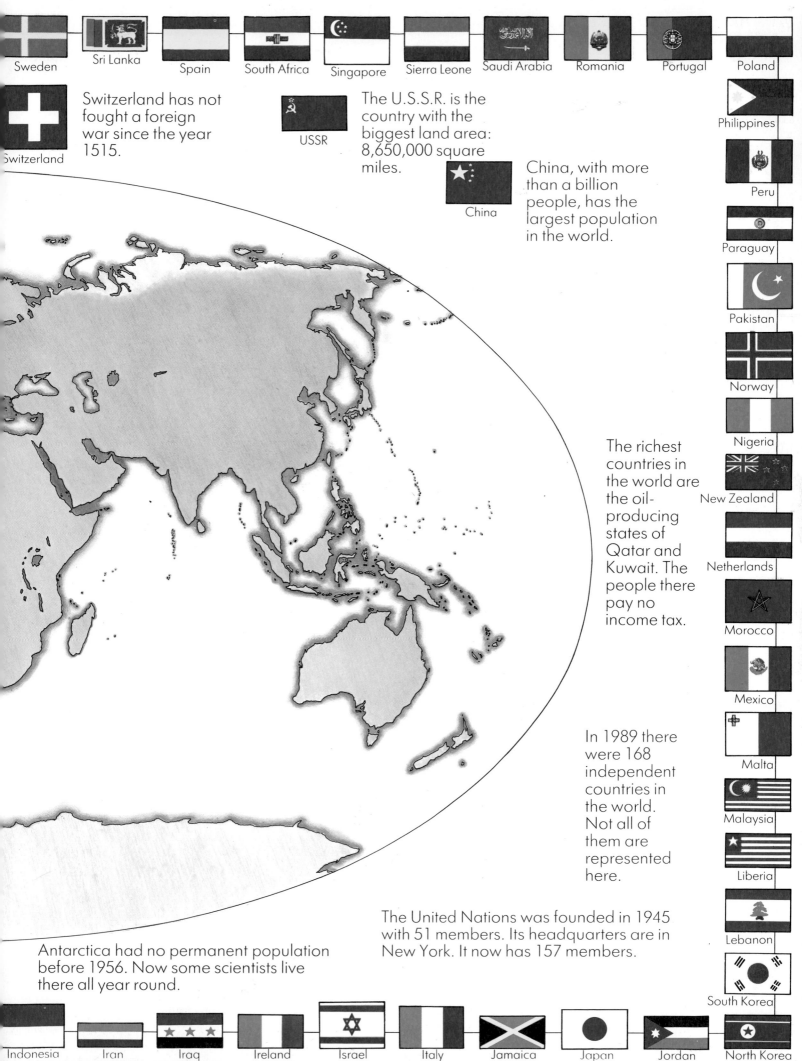

Sweden • Sri Lanka • Spain • South Africa • Singapore • Sierra Leone • Saudi Arabia • Romania • Portugal • Poland

Switzerland

Switzerland has not fought a foreign war since the year 1515.

USSR

The U.S.S.R. is the country with the biggest land area: 8,650,000 square miles.

China

China, with more than a billion people, has the largest population in the world.

Philippines

Peru

Paraguay

Pakistan

Norway

Nigeria

New Zealand

The richest countries in the world are the oil-producing states of Qatar and Kuwait. The people there pay no income tax.

Netherlands

Morocco

Mexico

Malta

Malaysia

In 1989 there were 168 independent countries in the world. Not all of them are represented here.

Liberia

Lebanon

Antarctica had no permanent population before 1956. Now some scientists live there all year round.

The United Nations was founded in 1945 with 51 members. Its headquarters are in New York. It now has 157 members.

South Korea

Indonesia • Iran • Iraq • Ireland • Israel • Italy • Jamaica • Japan • Jordan • North Korea

Towns and Cities

The Great Fire of London in 1666 destroyed 13,000 houses and 89 churches.

The town of Jericho is the oldest in the world. People have lived here for over 9,000 years.

London

Jericho

CITY FACTS

New York City is famed for its towering skyscrapers. The city was founded in 1625 by the Dutch, who called their settlement New Amsterdam.

More than 17 million people live in and around Mexico City. The Tokyo-Yokohama urban area has even more people — 29 million.

The highest capital city is La Paz in Bolivia, 12,000 feet above sea level.

Over 4,000 years ago the city of Mohenjo-Daro, close to the Indus River (modern Pakistan), was built with excellent drains and piped water. Nearly every house had a bathroom.

Manhattan Island was bought by the Dutch from the local Indians for a few beads and ribbons. Today it has the highest land values anywhere in the world.

castle

Many European towns grew up around forts and castles.

Syria's capital city, Damascus, has been inhabited for almost 4,500 years, making it the world's most ancient capital.

The Indians of Mesa Verde in the southwestern United States lived in cave-cities hollowed out of cliffs.

The Roman town of Pompeii was covered in ash in A.D. 79 when the volcano Vesuvius erupted. Streets and buildings preserved by the ash have now been uncovered for us to see.

Roman town

Mesa Verde

New York

Natural Wonders

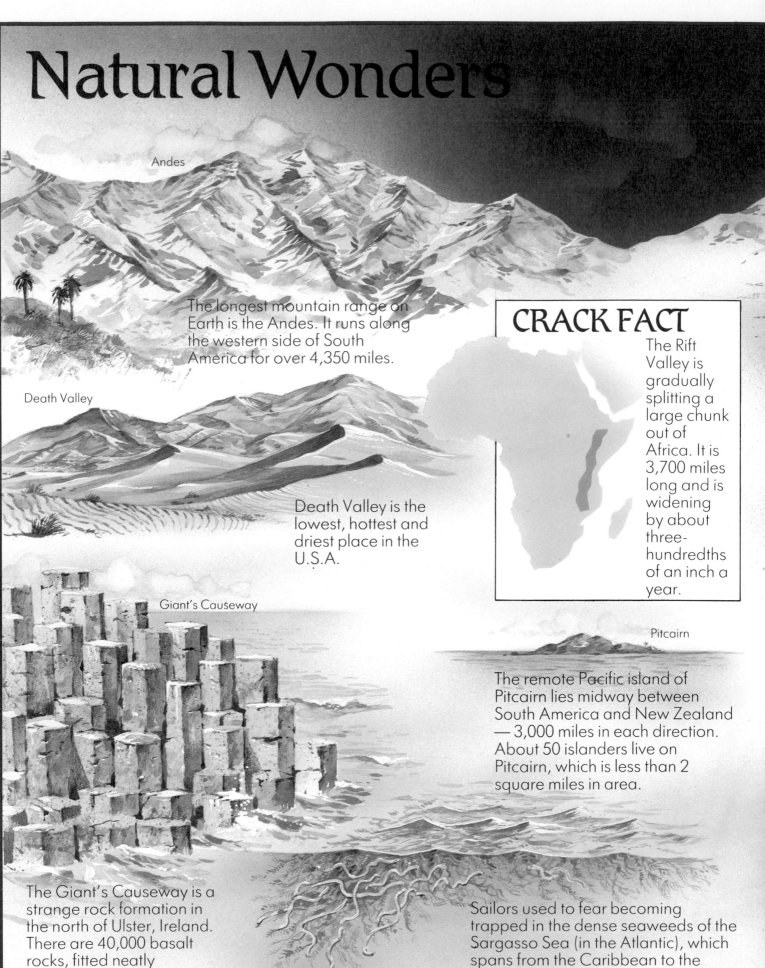

Andes

The longest mountain range on Earth is the Andes. It runs along the western side of South America for over 4,350 miles.

Death Valley

Death Valley is the lowest, hottest and driest place in the U.S.A.

CRACK FACT

The Rift Valley is gradually splitting a large chunk out of Africa. It is 3,700 miles long and is widening by about three-hundredths of an inch a year.

Giant's Causeway

Pitcairn

The remote Pacific island of Pitcairn lies midway between South America and New Zealand — 3,000 miles in each direction. About 50 islanders live on Pitcairn, which is less than 2 square miles in area.

The Giant's Causeway is a strange rock formation in the north of Ulster, Ireland. There are 40,000 basalt rocks, fitted neatly together in columns.

Sargasso Sea

Sailors used to fear becoming trapped in the dense seaweeds of the Sargasso Sea (in the Atlantic), which spans from the Caribbean to the Azores. Eels from the rivers of Europe make their way here to breed.

The Aurora Borealis, or Northern Lights, are brilliant light-shows in the sky caused by solar particles hitting the Earth's atmosphere.

Northern Lights

Mount Fuji

The snow-capped volcano Mount Fuji is Japan's most famous mountain. It last erupted in 1707.

Ayers Rock

Ayers Rock stands in the middle of Australia. It is 4 miles long and 1 1/2 miles wide.

The Rainbow Bridge in Utah, is the longest natural stone bridge in the world. It is 280 feet long and arches high above a stream.

Rainbow Arch

A famous mirage, or natural optical illusion, called the Fata Morgana, appears in the Strait of Messina between Italy and Sicily.

Fata Morgana

Between 15,000 and 40,000 years ago a huge iron meteorite hurtling through space crashed into the Earth. The impact gouged out Meteor Crater in Arizona. It is 4,000 feet across and 600 feet deep.

Meteor Crater

Petrified forests in Arizona are the fossilized remains of long-dead trees, turned to stone.

petrified forest

Australia's Great Barrier Reef is the largest structure ever made by living creatures. The reef contains 350 different corals, which have built a reef 1,200 miles long — long enough to stretch from New York to New Orleans.

Great Barrier Reef

Construction Marvels

The only construction built by people that is big enough to be seen from the Moon is the Great Wall of China. Over 1,500 miles long, it was built in the third century B.C. to protect China from invasion.

The Statue of Liberty stands on an island in New York harbor and is 300 feet tall. It was given to the United States by France in 1886.

The biggest Christian church in the world is the Basilica of St Peter in the Vatican City, completed in 1612.

The Humber Bridge in England has the longest single span in the world — 4,626 feet.

ENGINEERING WONDERS

King Louis XIV of France ordered 30,000 workers to build the Palace of Versailles. It took 50 years, beginning in 1661. There were 14,000 fountains in the gardens.

The Krak des Chevaliers in Syria is the largest Crusader castle. Within its massive walls, 2,000 soldiers could survive a year-long siege.

Joseph Paxton's Crystal Palace in London (1851) contained 293,000 panes of glass and 200 miles of ironwork. It was built in just eight months.

The longest road tunnel is the St. Gotthard Tunnel in Switzerland, at 10 miles.

A water-carrying tunnel supplying New York is almost 105 miles long — the longest in the world.

Sydney Harbor Bridge in Australia (1932) is almost 160 feet wide. Across it run two railroad tracks, eight road lanes, and special lanes for cyclists and pedestrians.

The heads of four U.S. presidents (George Washington, Thomas Jefferson, Theodore Roosevelt, and Abraham Lincoln) are carved in granite on Mount Rushmore, South Dakota. Each head is as big as a five-story building.

The Sears Tower in Chicago is the tallest building in the world. It has 110 stories and is 1,453 feet high. There is room for over 16,000 office workers — with a window for almost everyone.

The world's tallest structure is a TV and radio mast in Poland which is 2,120 feet high.

The world's first skyscraper, designed by William LeBaron Jenney, was the Home Insurance Building in Chicago (1885).

THE SEVEN WONDERS OF THE ANCIENT WORLD ARE . . .
1   The Pyramids at Giza, Egypt.
2   The Hanging Gardens of Babylon.
3   The Temple of Artemis at Ephesus.
4   The Statue of Zeus at Olympia.
5   The Mausoleum (tomb of King Mausolus) at Halicarnassus.
6   The Colossus of Rhodes.
7   The Pharos (Lighthouse) of Alexandria.
Today, only the Pyramids can still be seen.

The 630-foot Gateway to the West in St. Louis, Missouri, is the tallest monument in the United States.

The Pyramids of ancient Egypt were built around 2600 B.C. The largest is the Great Pyramid of Cheops which (having lost its topmost stones) is 450 feet high. It contains over two million stones, each weighing around two tons.

There are ancient Aztec pyramids in Central America.

The Eiffel Tower in Paris, France, was completed in 1889. More than 7,000 tons of iron were used to build it.

Uncovering the Past

In 1968 archaeologists in China found two royal tombs. Their rich treasures included jade suits in which Prince Lui Sheng and his wife Tu Wan were buried over 2,000 years ago. Each suit was made of over 2,000 plates of thin jade, sewn together with gold wire.

The only tomb of an ancient Egyptian pharaoh discovered with all its treasures was that of Tutankhamun, found by Howard Carter in 1922 in Egypt's Valley of the Kings. Inside were four rooms filled with over 5,000 objects.

jade suit

Stonehenge

People who find out about the past by digging up remains are called archaeologists. Early archaeologists looked mainly for treasure. The first to value everyday objects as well was Sir Flinders Petrie (1853–1942).

Tutankhamun

archaeologists

60

Stonehenge, the most famous prehistoric stone monument in Europe, was built between 2800 and 1500 B.C. Its biggest stones weigh around 50 tons.

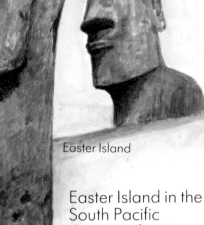

Easter Island

Easter Island in the South Pacific Ocean is famous for its enormous stone heads. There are over 600 of them, probably made between A.D. 1000 and 1600, although nobody knows why.

The first tools used by humans were made of stone, bone, and wood. Among the earliest are small stones with a sharpened edge for cutting or scraping.

early tools

The oldest "human" footprints known were discovered at Laetoli, Tanzania, by Mary Leakey in 1978. The three sets of prints, preserved in volcanic ash, were made by humanlike creatures when walking in Africa 3.7 million years ago.

Mary Leakey

Ancient Civilizations

EGYPT

Egyptian civilization began 5,000 years ago beside the River Nile, which flooded each year to leave behind rich, black, fertile, soil.

The Egyptians preserved dead bodies as "mummies." They also mummified cats, dogs, baboons, crocodiles, fish, and birds.

About 3000 B.C. the Egyptians began writing in pictures called hieroglyphics.

CHINA

China has the world's oldest civilization, with a written history dating back 3,500 years.

The earliest Chinese towns grew up on the banks of the Yellow River.

The Chinese call their land Zhongguo, meaning Middle Country — the center of the Earth.

Chinese inventions include porcelain, paper, the compass, and silk-making.

paper making

ARABIA

The Arabs were among the first people to study the stars. There were astronomical observatories at Baghdad and Damascus about A.D. 1000.

Many of the brightest stars in the sky have names given them by Arab astronomers.

Our word "algebra" is also Arabic and comes from an Arab mathematics book of A.D. 825.

The numbers we use are Arabic. The Arabs learned the number-signs from Indian traders and scholars.

GREECE

Greek civilization began about 2000 B.C.

The Greeks lived in small city states. One state, Athens, was the birthplace of democratic government.

The population of ancient Greece was under two million. Yet Greek culture formed the basis of Western civilization.

ROME

Legend has it that Rome was founded by the twin brothers Romulus and Remus in 752 B.C. The city grew up on seven hills along the River Tiber.

At its peak, in the A.D. 100s, Rome's empire covered half of Europe, much of the Middle East, and North Africa.

The Romans had so many holidays that in the A.D. 100s the emperor limited them to just 135 days in a year!

Wars and Battles

Sailing ships were first armed with cannon firing broadsides in around 1500. By 1800 a first-rate warship carried over 90 guns. Two thousand trees were needed to build such a ship.

WAR FACTS

The longest war was the Hundred Years' War between England and France. It began in 1338 and lasted until 1453.

The shortest important war was the Six Day War between Israelis and Arabs, which lasted from June 5th to 10th 1967.

A much shorter "war" took place in 1896 between Britain and Zanzibar. It lasted 38 minutes, and consisted of a naval bombardment.

The most destructive war was World War II (1939–45). Almost 55 million people were killed.

When attacking a fort, Roman soldiers made a "shell" with their shields for protection against arrows, rocks, and other missiles. All four sides of the *testudo* or "tortoise" could also be shielded.

A first-century Roman legion numbered 5,500 soldiers, all Roman citizens. There were about 30 legions in the Roman Army. Most of the soldiers were infantrymen.

The first underwater attack by submarine was made in 1775. During the Revolutionary War, a tiny American submarine tried to sink a British ship, but failed.

The world's largest submarines are the Soviet Navy's Typhoon class boats, 25,000 tons and 558 feet long.

In medieval times a knight's armor weighed around 110 pounds. He needed a powerful warhorse to carry him into battle.

The Samurai of Japan refused to use firearms, calling the new invention a "coward's weapon." They preferred their curved swords made of the finest steel.

The first tanks rolled into battle in 1916 during World War I.

The American Civil War lasted from 1861 to 1865. The turning point was the Battle of Gettysburg (1863), won by the North. Both sides lost about 23,000 men in the battle.

US Civil War

The Japanese carrier-borne air attack on the U.S. naval base of Pearl Harbor took place on December 7, 1941.

The first long-range missile was Germany's V2 rocket, used during World War II. Each rocket traveled faster than the speed of sound.

Pearl Harbor

BATTLE FACTS

During World War I (1914–18) more than a million soldiers were killed or wounded at the first Battle of the Somme in 1916.

During the Battle of Stalingrad (1942–43), 2.5 million people are believed to have died.

The longest siege in history was by German armies surrounding Leningrad, U.S.S.R.: it lasted from August 1941 to January 1944.

The largest invasion of all time happened on June 6, 1944. In four weeks one million Allied troops landed in France. More than 700 ships and 4,000 landing craft took part.

Famous Leaders

Solomon (about 1015 B.C. — about 977 B.C.) King of Israel, son of David. Known for his wisdom and wealth. Under Solomon, Israel reached the peak of its greatness.

Alexander the Great (356–323 B.C.) One of the world's greatest generals. Ruler of Macedon (Greece), conquered much of the civilized world.

Gaius Julius Caesar (about 101–44 B.C.) Roman soldier and statesman, who made Rome the capital of a mighty empire. Conquered much of Europe.

Cleopatra (69–30 B.C.) Ruler of Egypt. Last of dynasty (ruling family) founded 323 B.C. by Ptolemy. Poisoned herself after death of lover Mark Antony.

Boudicca or **Boadicea** (died A.D. 62) Queen of the Iceni, ancient British tribe of East Anglia. Led a revolt against Roman rule in Britain.

Charlemagne (742–814) King of the Franks, crowned Holy Roman Emperor in 800. Built up a united Christian Empire in western Europe.

Alfred the Great (849–899) King of the West Saxons. Reorganized army, built a fleet, made wise laws, encouraged learning.

William the Conqueror (1027–87) Duke of Normandy and King of England. Invaded England in 1066. Built castles, took ownership of all land.

Genghis Khan (1162–1227) Mongol conqueror, founder of the largest land empire in history. At his death, his empire stretched from China to European Russia.

Henry the Eighth (1491–1547) King of England. Famous for his six wives. Created the Church of England with himself at its head.

Elizabeth (1533–1603) Queen of England. Encouraged exploration by English seafarers and inspired defeat of Spanish Armada (1588).

Akbar (1542–1605) Mogul emperor of India. Became famous for his justice and religious tolerance. Reformed taxes and laws.

Louis the Fourteenth (1638–1715) "Sun King" of France. Absolute monarch. Reigned for 72 years. His court was the most magnificent in Europe. Built the Palace of Versailles.

George Washington (1732–99) First President of the United States (1789–96). Became commander-in-chief of American forces during Revolutionary War (1775–83).

Napoleon Bonaparte (1769–1821) Emperor of France and military genius. Conquered Egypt, Italy, Spain, Netherlands, and most of central Europe. Defeated in 1815 at Battle of Waterloo.

Giuseppe Garibaldi (1807–82) Italy's national hero. Fought to unite states of Italy into one nation. In 1860 conquered Naples and made Victor Emmanuel first king of united Italy.

Abraham Lincoln (1809–65) President of the United States. Opposed slavery in Southern states. Led Union to victory in Civil War (1861–65), saving the nation from splitting apart.

Otto von Bismarck (1815–98) Founder of modern Germany. Worked to unite German states under Prussia's leadership. In 1871 became first Chancellor of the new German Empire.

Victoria (1819–1901) Longest reigning monarch in British history (nearly 64 years). Ruled over an empire which included about a quarter of the Earth's land and people.

Mohandas Karamchand Gandhi (1869–1948) Known as Mahatma. Led movement for Indian independence from British rule, by non-violent means. Lived simply, believed in religious tolerance.

Lenin Born Vladimir Ilich Ulyanov (1870–1924) Leader of Russian Revolution and founder of first Communist state. Followed revolutionary ideas of Karl Marx. Seized power in Russia in 1917.

Winston Churchill (1874–1965) Prime Minister of Great Britain during World War II. Worked with U.S. President Franklin Roosevelt to achieve Allied victory in 1945.

Adolf Hitler (1889–1945) German Nazi Party founder and leader. Became German dictator (Führer) 1934. Invaded Poland 1939, thus starting World War II. Millions of people, mostly Jews, killed on his orders

Mao Ze-dong (1893–1976) Chinese Communist leader. Defeated Nationalists to make China Communist, 1949. Started "Cultural Revolution" in 1960s to remove all traces of China's past.

Explorers

Marco Polo was only 17 when he traveled overland from Italy to China in 1271 with his father and uncle. The Chinese ruler, Kublai Khan, sent Marco on business throughout China. The Polos did not return home for 24 years.

Marco Polo

EXPLORING FEATS

About 2500 B.C. the Egyptians sailed through the Red Sea to explore the "Land of Punt" — probably modern Somalia.

In 480 B.C. the Phoenician Hanno sailed out of the Mediterranean to explore the coast of West Africa.

Even before the Vikings sailed to North America around A.D. 1000, an Irish monk named Brendan may have sailed there in about A.D. 570.

Polynesian sailors crossed the Pacific Ocean to reach New Zealand during the A.D. 900s.

Ibn Battuta, an Arab traveler, visited West Africa, the Middle East, India, China, and Southeast Asia from 1325–1354. Altogether he traveled 75,000 miles in 30 years.

Vasco da Gamma was the first European to sail around Africa and on to India, in 1497–8.

David Livingstone

David Livingstone was the first European to discover the Victoria Falls in Africa, and searched for the source of the River Nile. In 1869 H.M. Stanley went to look for Livingstone, who was feared lost. He found him near Lake Tanganyika in 1871.

Cartier

In 1535 the French explorer Jacques Cartier was the first European to discover the St. Lawrence River in Canada. He traveled upstream to an Indian village on the site of the modern city of Montreal.

James Cook (1728–79) was a great ocean navigator. He was the first European to sail into Antarctic waters, the first to visit Hawaii, the first to chart the Great Barrier Reef, and the first to land on Vancouver Island.

Cook

The Portuguese Ferdinand Magellan led the first voyage around the world, 1519–22. He was the first European to sail across the Pacific Ocean, but was killed in the Philippines. One ship of his fleet (out of five) reached home.

The first European to see Australia was probably Willem Janz of Holland in 1606. Another Dutch navigator, Abel Tasman, discovered Tasmania and New Zealand in 1642.

Meriwether Lewis and William Clark traveled 8,000 miles from the Mississippi River to the Pacific coast of the United States, 1804–06.

The first explorer to prove that Lake Victoria was the source of the River Nile was John Hanning Speke, in 1863.

The first explorers to reach the North Pole were Robert Peary and Matthew Henson of the U.S.A. in 1909.

Columbus

Christopher Columbus sighted America in 1492, but thought he had reached Asia. He crossed the Atlantic four times, still seeking a new trade route to the East.

The first people to reach the South Pole were Roald Amundsen's Norwegian expedition in 1911, just ahead of R.F. Scott's British party. The Antarctic continent was crossed overland for the first time in 1958 by a British Commonwealth expedition led by Vivian Fuchs.

Scott

Amundsen

Science Marvels

Everything is made of atoms. Atoms are very tiny. One atom is about a million times smaller than the thickness of a human hair.

Each atom is made of tiny particles spinning around a center or nucleus — rather like tiny planets orbiting a tiny sun.

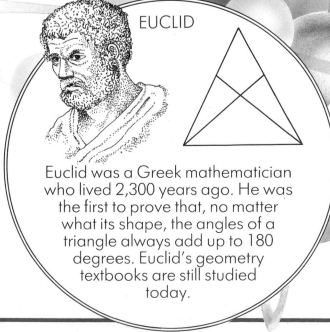

EUCLID

Euclid was a Greek mathematician who lived 2,300 years ago. He was the first to prove that, no matter what its shape, the angles of a triangle always add up to 180 degrees. Euclid's geometry textbooks are still studied today.

GALILEO

Galileo Galilei (1564–1642) was one of the first real scientists, carrying out experiments to find how things happened. Using a home-made telescope, he was the first person to see mountains on the Moon. He also discovered sunspots and four moons of Jupiter.

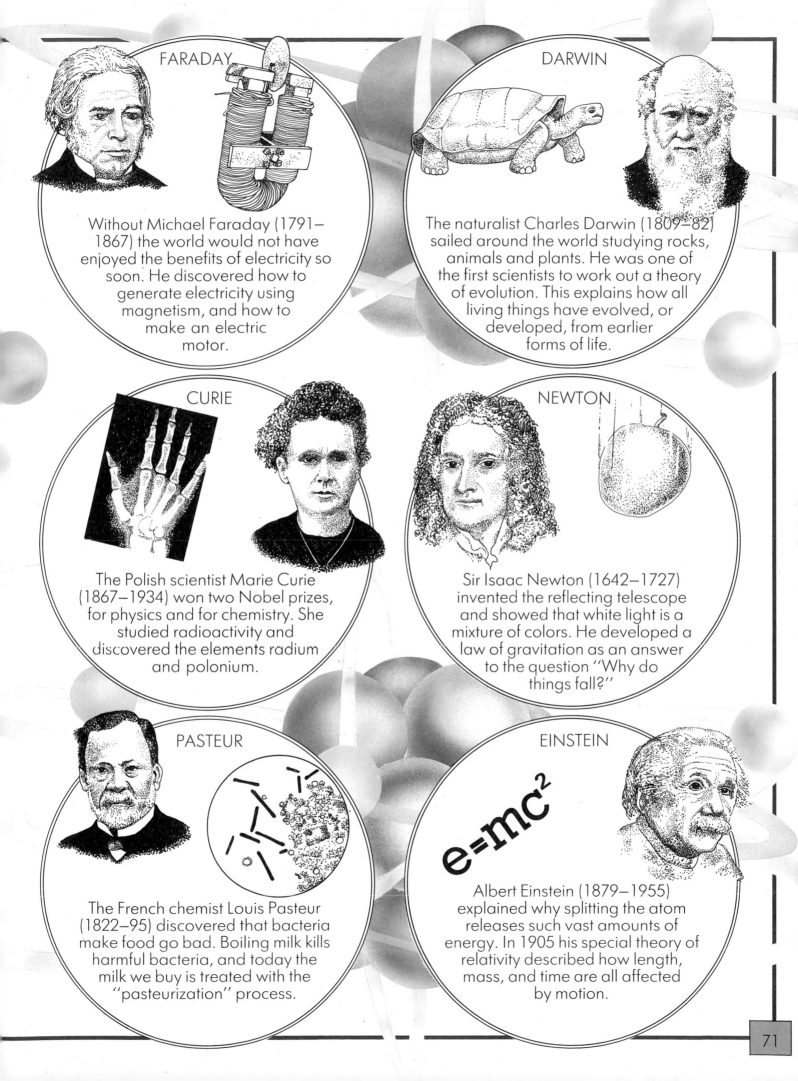

FARADAY

Without Michael Faraday (1791–1867) the world would not have enjoyed the benefits of electricity so soon. He discovered how to generate electricity using magnetism, and how to make an electric motor.

DARWIN

The naturalist Charles Darwin (1809–82) sailed around the world studying rocks, animals and plants. He was one of the first scientists to work out a theory of evolution. This explains how all living things have evolved, or developed, from earlier forms of life.

CURIE

The Polish scientist Marie Curie (1867–1934) won two Nobel prizes, for physics and for chemistry. She studied radioactivity and discovered the elements radium and polonium.

NEWTON

Sir Isaac Newton (1642–1727) invented the reflecting telescope and showed that white light is a mixture of colors. He developed a law of gravitation as an answer to the question "Why do things fall?"

PASTEUR

The French chemist Louis Pasteur (1822–95) discovered that bacteria make food go bad. Boiling milk kills harmful bacteria, and today the milk we buy is treated with the "pasteurization" process.

EINSTEIN

$$e = mc^2$$

Albert Einstein (1879–1955) explained why splitting the atom releases such vast amounts of energy. In 1905 his special theory of relativity described how length, mass, and time are all affected by motion.

71

Inventions and Discoveries

The wheel was one of the most important human inventions. Wheels seem to have been used before 3000 B.C. in several different places. The first wheels were solid.

People in ancient India had drains and bathrooms 4,500 years ago. But flush toilets came later. The modern toilet or water closet dates from the 1770s, and was designed by Joseph Bramah.

INVENTION FIRSTS

The earliest machines were the wedge, the lever, and the ramp or inclined plane. They were being used 100,000 years ago.

Metal coins were first made 2,500 years ago by the Lydians, a people living in Asia Minor.

The magnetic compass is a Chinese invention. It was in use in Europe by the 1100s.

Printing with movable type, using a press, was invented in Germany about 1440 by Johannes Gutenberg.

People first wrote with pencils made of graphite in wooden holders in 1565.

Louis Lenormand demonstrated the use of the first parachute in 1783.

The first battery for producing electric current was made by an Italian named Alessandro Volta in 1800.

The zipper was first thought of by an American named Whitcomb Judson in 1891.

Frozen foods were first sold in the 1920s. An American named Clarence Birdseye got the idea after a winter fishing trip when his catch froze solid on the ice. People had known for many years that snow and ice kept food fresh. Refrigerated ships were first built to carry meat during the 1800s.

0 + 1 = ?

The symbol 0, meaning zero or nothing, was first used in mathematics in Asia more than 1,200 years ago. The Chinese used decimals long before 1400 B.C.

The first electric light bulbs began to replace gas lamps in the 1880s. They were airless glass globes containing a very thin carbon strip which glowed brightly when electricity passed through it.

The first photograph was taken in 1822 by Joseph Niepce of France. It was made on a glass plate.

The French chemist Hippolyte Mège-Mouriés developed a method for making margarine in 1870.

The telephone was invented by Alexander Graham Bell in 1876.

Guglielmo Marconi's first radio signals (1895) were sent in telegraph code.

The world's first electronic computer was called ENIAC. It was built in the U.S.A. in 1946.

The microwave oven was invented in 1948.

The first laser was made in 1960 by the American Theodore H. Maiman. The light beam from a laser contains light of only one color.

By flying a kite during a thunderstorm in 1752, Benjamin Franklin showed that lightning was a form of electricity. Lightning struck a metal rod hanging from the kite and passed down the string to a metal key he was holding. (**This was a very dangerous experiment!**)

People were first able to buy canned foods in the 1820s. But no-one had invented a can-opener. In the 1860s an unknown inventor designed a can-opener to cut the top off a can.

The first-ever sound recording was made by Thomas Alva Edison in 1877. He recorded "*Mary had a little lamb*" on his phonograph machine.

The first vacuum cleaner to suck up dirt was invented by Hubert Booth in 1901. He tested the idea on a carpet, sucking with his mouth through his handkerchief.

In 1898 Valdemar Poulsen of Denmark invented a machine for recording sound magnetically on steel wire — the "telegraphone."

Science Rules

ATOMS

The ancient Greeks thought nothing could be smaller than an atom. But the atom can be split into tinier particles. The nucleus or center of an atom is 10,000 times smaller than the atom itself. Atoms can be seen only through special microscopes.

MOLECULES

Atoms join together to form molecules. A page in this book is about 100,000 molecules thick. If you tore up a sheet of paper into the tiniest pieces, each piece is still paper. If each paper molecule were to be broken apart, it would no longer be paper. It would just be a collection of atoms.

ELEMENTS

An element is a substance which has only one kind of atom in it. There are more than 100 elements, not all of them found naturally on Earth. The commonest elements are oxygen, nitrogen, and hydrogen. Gold is the "stretchiest" element; a single gram can be drawn into a thread over a mile long.

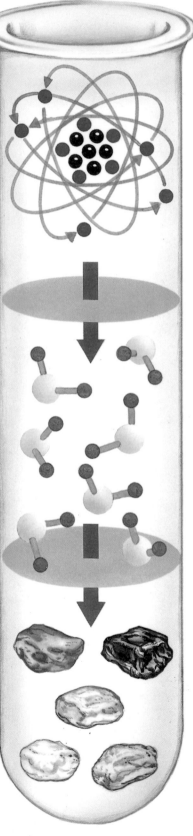

SOUND

A Saturn 5 Moon rocket made the loudest engine noise ever measured: 210 decibels. There is no noise at all on the Moon, since there is no air there for sound waves to travel through. The speed of sound is about 1,115 feet a second.

LIGHT

Nothing moves faster than light, which travels at almost 186,000 miles a second. Light is a form of energy, and our light comes from the Sun. The brightest artificial light is laser light. Light is made up of a mixture of colors. The primary colors of white light are red, green, and blue.

HEAT

Heat is another form of energy. When a substance is heated, its molecules move about faster. When it is cooled, they move more slowly. The coldest anything can be is "absolute zero" (−495°F.). The hottest place on Earth is 136°F. Iron melts at 2,730°F. The center of the Sun is 27 million degrees.

ELECTRICITY

Although known about since ancient times, electricity was not used to light and heat buildings before the 1800s. The first electric light bulb was invented in 1878. The first city power station was opened in New York in 1882.

MAGNETISM

The Earth itself is an enormous magnet. All magnets have two poles, near their ends. We call them North and South. A North pole will attract a South pole, but repel another North pole. The first people to use magnets in compasses were the Chinese, about 1,000 years ago.

ENERGY AND MOTION

To start a weight swinging on the end of a cord, it needs to be pushed. The force of your push makes the weight move. You have transferred energy from your body to the swinging pendulum. Matter can be changed into energy, and energy can be changed into matter.

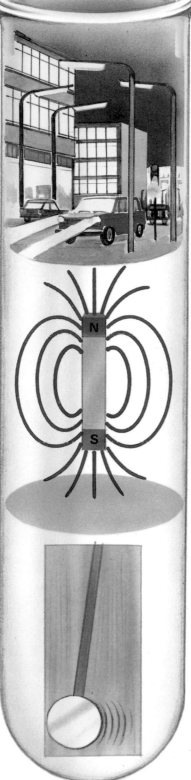

GAS

A gas has no volume or shape. Most gases are invisible because their molecules are spread very thinly. If a gas is heated, it expands or takes up more room. A balloon filled with hot air rises because it is less dense than the surrounding air.

LIQUID

A liquid (such as water) has volume, but no shape. If a liquid is cooled, it can become a solid. For example, water freezes to ice. When water is heated, it becomes a gas called water vapor. Water is unusual because it is one of only two liquid minerals. The other one is mercury.

SOLID

In a solid, the molecules are held tightly together. This gives the solid both volume and shape. When heated to its melting point, a solid becomes a liquid. Ice, for instance, melts to water. Matter can exist as solid, liquid, or gas.

Medical Miracles

thermometer

The first stethoscope was made by René Laennec in 1816. He got the idea from using a rolled paper tube to listen to a person's heartbeats.

stethoscope

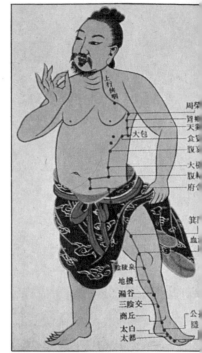

acupuncture

thermometer

stethoscope

The thermometer was invented in 1592 by Galileo. But a more reliable type for medical use was developed in 1654 in Italy.

Among the earliest doctors were the physicians of ancient Egypt and China. More than 3,000 years ago, Chinese surgeons performed operations using acupuncture needles as pain killers.

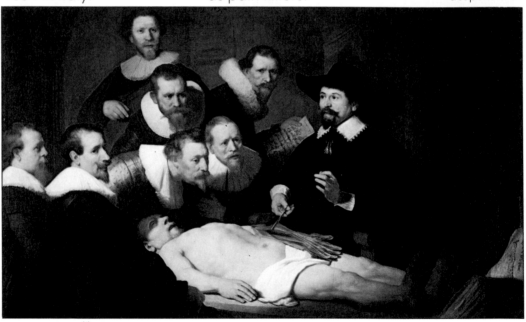

The Anatomy Lesson by Rembrandt (1632)

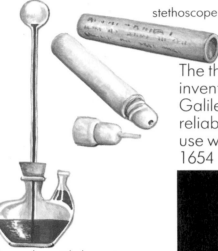

People with hearing problems used to hold ear trumpets up to their ear. A comfortable hearing aid was first developed in the 1930s.

Glasses were worn in the Middle Ages. The first ones had only a single lens. Pairs of lenses clipped onto the nose were worn in the 1500s.

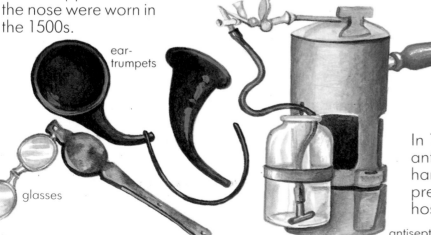

ear-trumpets

glasses

Until the 1600s, the Church forbade people to dissect, or cut up, human bodies for scientific study. So many dissections had to be carried out in secret.

In 1865 Joseph Lister used antiseptic carbolic sprays to kill harmful bacteria, and so prevent infection inside hospitals.

antiseptic carbolic spray

William Morton

The first operation performed with the use of ether as an anesthetic took place in Massachusetts in 1846. The ether was given by a dentist, William Morton.

X-rays were discovered by Wilhelm von Roentgen in 1895. For the first time, doctors could see what was going on inside a patient's body.

MEDICAL FIRSTS

The Greek doctor Hippocrates (born 460 B.C.) is called the Father of Medicine. He taught doctors to observe scientifically.

False teeth were worn by the ancient Etruscans about 700 B.C. They were made of bone or ivory (or they used the teeth of other people).

In 1543 Andreas Vesalius published the first scientific book on the anatomy of the human body.

Artificial limbs were made as long ago as 500 B.C. The French surgeon Ambroise Paré was the first to make limbs that looked lifelike, in the 1560s.

illustration from Harvey's book on blood circulation.

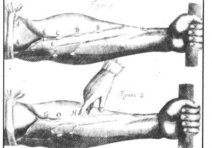

William Harvey was the first person to show that blood was pumped around the body by the heart. This was in 1619.

The dental drill was invented in 1790 in the U.S.A.

In the 1790s, Edward Jenner immunized a boy against smallpox by injecting him with a dose of cowpox (a less serious illness). This was the first successful vaccination. Pasteur used inoculation to cure rabies in 1885.

The founder of modern nursing was Florence Nightingale. She was shocked by the terrible conditions she found when nursing soldiers during the Crimean War of 1854–56.

The first vaccine against polio was developed by Dr. Jonas Salk in the early 1950s.

The first heart transplant operation was performed by Christiaan Barnard in South Africa in 1967.

The first antibiotic, used to kill harmful germs, was penicillin. It was found by Alexander Fleming in 1928, but not made for medical use until 1941, thanks to the work of Howard Florey and Ernst Chain.

The first operation to replace a human heart with an artificial heart was in 1982.

Travel

Just one of Ferdinand Magellan's five ships sailed home in 1522 after the first round-the-world voyage — 50,000 miles in three years. Joshua Slocum, the first lone yachtsman to sail around the world, also took three years, 1895–98.

In 1889 U.S. journalist Nellie Bly journeyed around the world in 72 days 6 hours 11 minutes, traveling mostly by ship and train.

American Wiley Post flew solo around the world in 1933. It took him 7 days 18 hours 49 minutes.

The first astronaut to orbit the Earth, Yuri Gagarin, took just 108 minutes from takeoff to landing.

The U.S. Space Shuttle first flew in 1981. It can lift 64,000 pounds into orbit.

Space Shuttle

SPACE TRAVEL FACTS

The U.S. Space Shuttle lands on the world's longest runway, 7 miles long, at Edwards Air Force Base, California.

If the British space plane HOTOL were built for commercial use, it could fly from Britain to Australia in less than an hour.

The American Apollo Moon rockets were blasted from the Earth at a top speed of about 24,000 mph — almost 20 times faster than the Concorde can fly.

TRAVEL FACTS

The world's largest airport is at Riyadh, the capital of Saudi Arabia. The busiest airport is O'Hare, in Chicago, where a plane lands or takes off every 40 seconds.

Every year more than 500 million passengers fly on the world's scheduled airline services.

The U.S.A. is the country with the most motor vehicles. There is one vehicle for every 1.5 people. In Bangladesh, there is one motor vehicle for every 1,600 people.

The U.S.S.R. has the greatest length of canals in the world, with 85,000 miles.

In China, there are thought to be 210 million bicycles: one for every five people.

The world's largest airline is the Soviet state airline, Aeroflot.

Road Transportation

The first wheels turned with the axle. Later, lighter spoked wheels that turned around the axle were invented and used on chariots.

The first vehicles were wooden sledges. For moving heavy loads, people used log rollers.

Until 1896 in Britain a man with a red flag had to walk in front of a car to warn people of its approach.

In 1886 Karl Benz was granted a patent for a three-wheeled "motor-wagon." Two months later Gottlieb Daimler demonstrated his four-wheeler.

The highwheeler of the 1870s had the biggest wheel of any bicycle. It was the racing bike of its day.

Henry Ford's Model T took 12½ hours to assemble in 1908, but just 90 minutes by 1914.

The 1970s Porsche 917 was the most powerful car, and the fastest car going, capable of 300 mph.

The first modern highways were the Italian "autostradas" and the German "autobahns" of the 1920s and 1930s.

The Volkswagen "Beetle" was first built in 1938.

Oxen were used to pull carts in ancient times.

The Romans built the first big network of paved roads. By the A.D. 200s over 50,000 miles of roads linked Rome to the farthest parts of its empire.

The first passenger coach service began in Paris in the 1660s. Coaches on long-distance routes stopped at "stages" to change horses, and were therefore called "stagecoaches."

Small carriages, called cabriolets, or cabs, were popular in the 1800s. Some were used as taxis are used today.

The first person to make a steam engine drive a wheeled vehicle was Nicolas Cugnot of France in 1769. Its top speed was just over 2 mph.

The Pony Express mail riders galloped across America. The 2,000-mile route had 190 stations. The first trip, in 1860, took ten days.

Travelers had to pay to use toll roads at barriers called turnpikes. The first American toll road was opened in Pennsylvania in 1794.

The first motorcycle was built by Gottlieb Daimler in 1885. Its top speed was less than 12 mph. The fastest modern road bike can do over 175 mph.

The heaviest truck would be dwarfed by the giant earthmover "Big Muskie," which weighs almost 11,000 tons.

ROAD FACTS

The "cat's eye," for showing the line of a road at night, was invented by Percy Shaw in 1934.

Traffic lights were first used in Detroit, in 1919.

The first important car race was in 1895, when 27 cars raced for over 600 miles in France. The winner took 2 days 48 minutes, at an average speed of just under 20 mph.

Parking meters first appeared in the U.S.A. in the 1930s.

The lead added to petrol is harmful to health. Today, drivers are switching to lead-free fuel.

Rail

The first public steam railroad was the Stockton and Darlington Railway, 1825. George Stephenson drove the first train, which pulled 33 wagons at a top speed of 15 mph (downhill).

The biggest locomotives ever were the American Big Boys. Built in the early 1940s, these monsters were 130 feet long and weighed 534 tons.

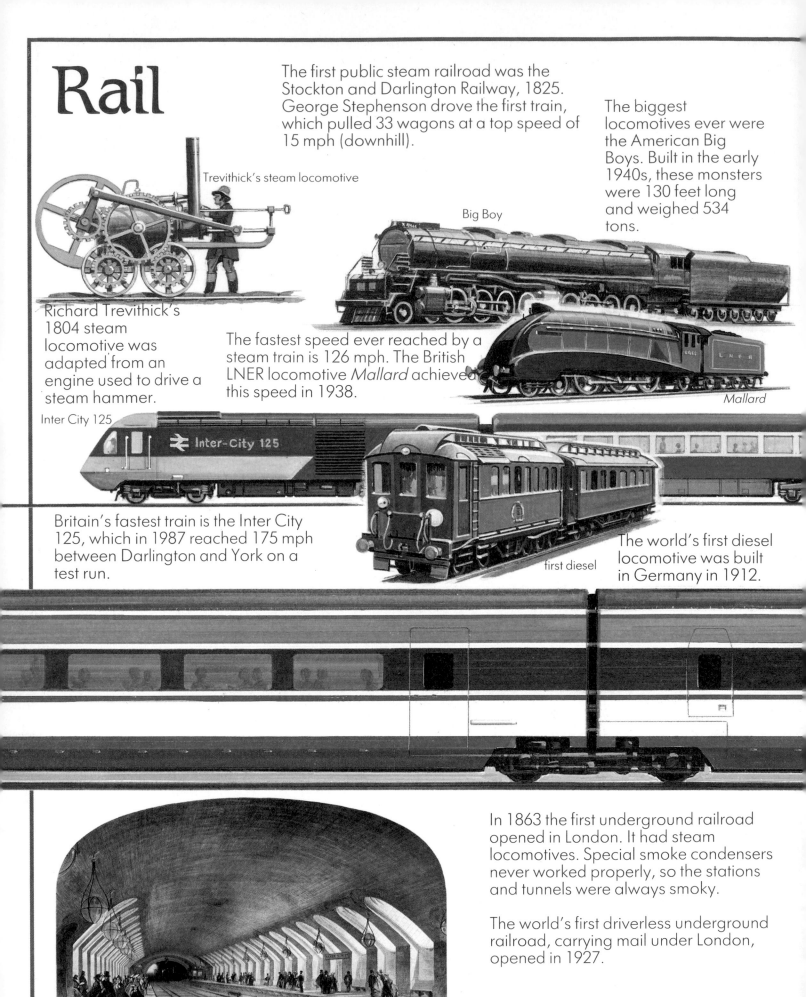

Trevithick's steam locomotive

Big Boy

Richard Trevithick's 1804 steam locomotive was adapted from an engine used to drive a steam hammer.

The fastest speed ever reached by a steam train is 126 mph. The British LNER locomotive *Mallard* achieved this speed in 1938.

Mallard

Inter City 125

Britain's fastest train is the Inter City 125, which in 1987 reached 175 mph between Darlington and York on a test run.

first diesel

The world's first diesel locomotive was built in Germany in 1912.

In 1863 the first underground railroad opened in London. It had steam locomotives. Special smoke condensers never worked properly, so the stations and tunnels were always smoky.

The world's first driverless underground railroad, carrying mail under London, opened in 1927.

London Underground

monorail

The first monorail was the Listowel and Ballybunion Railway in Ireland (1889).

rack railroad

RAIL FACTS

The world's longest passenger train ran in the Netherlands in 1988. It had 60 carriages and stretched for a mile.

The highest standard gauge railroad is the Central Railroad of Peru, which climbs three miles above sea level.

The world's biggest station is Grand Central in New York City.

The world speed record for trains is held by two French electric locomotives which hauled three-carriage trains at 205 mph in 1955.

An experimental Maglev train in Japan and a West German test train have each traveled at more than 250 mph.

The longest rail journey starts at Moscow and finishes at Nakhodka in Soviet Asia. The 6,000-mile journey takes over eight days.

The steepest rack railroad is the Mount Pilatus railroad in Switzerland (1889) with a maximum gradient of 1 in 2.1.

The fastest express trains are the French TGVs and the Japanese Bullets. The TGVs average over 125 mph.

French TGV

The rail link in the Channel Tunnel between Britain and France will be 30 miles long, 23 miles under water.

Sea

In 1989 the speedboat *Gentry Eagle* crossed the Atlantic in a record 62 hours 7 minutes and 47 seconds.

speedboat

The largest liner ever built was the *Queen Elizabeth*, over 85,000 tons and 1,030 feet long.

liner

The biggest ship ever was the tanker *Seawise Giant* (1976–88), which was 1,285 feet long and 565,000 tons.

tanker

yacht

SHIP FACTS

The earliest ships were log rafts paddled by hand. By about 3000 B.C. sails were used to catch the wind.

Christopher Columbus sailed to America in 1492 in a three-masted carrack, the *Santa Maria*, about 80 tons and 85 feet long.

The *Mary Rose*, a galleon built in 1510 for King Henry the Eighth of England, sank in 1545, and lay for 437 years on the ocean-bed until raised in 1982.

The first nuclear-powered ship was the Soviet ice-breaker *Lenin* of 1957.

The first steamship to cross the Atlantic (using sails part of the way) was the *Savannah*, in 1819.

The first yacht to sail around the world was the schooner *Nancy Dawson*, 1847–50.

SHIP RECORDS

The biggest sailing ship was the *France II* (5,800 tons, 416 feet long), launched in 1911.

The largest battleships ever built were Japan's World War II giants *Yamato* and *Musashi* (73,977 tons).

The fast sailing ships, called clippers, crossed the Atlantic in 12 days during the 1800s.

In 1947 Thor Heyerdahl crossed the Pacific on a balsawood raft called *Kon-Tiki*, covering 4,220 miles in 101 days.

The largest Chinese junk was the *Cheng Ho*, built about 1420. It was 3,150 tons and 538 feet long, and is thought to have had nine masts.

The *Titanic* (46,000 tons), largest liner of her day, sank in three hours after hitting an iceberg on her maiden voyage from Southampton to New York, in April 1912.

The ship with the most sails was the 18th-century East Indiaman *Essex*, with a set of 63.

sailing ship

Viking longships were the finest ships of northern Europe between the late 700s and late 1000s.

Viking longboat

paddle steamer

The first steamships, such as the *Charlotte Dundas* (1802), were driven by paddlewheels.

The first hovercraft was the SR-N1, 1959. The fastest, reaching 102 mph in 1980, was a U.S. Navy hovercraft.

hovercraft

hydrofoil

multi-hull boat

The multi-hulled vessel (catamaran or trimaran) is an ancient form of sailing craft, and was used by Pacific islanders.

reed boat

The Egyptians used reed boats 6,000 years ago. Reed boats are also sailed by Bolivian Indians on Lake Titicaca.

The world's fastest hydrofoil is the Royal Canadian Navy's *Bras d'Or*, with a top speed of 61 knots (70 mph).

The official highest speed on water is 317 mph, reached by K. P. Warby of Australia in 1978.

The biggest air-cushion vehicle (hovercraft) is the British SR-N4 (305 tons), which carries over 400 passengers.

The longest liner is the *Norway* (formerly *France*), launched in 1962, at 1,035 feet.

In the Air

FLYING FACTS

The Chinese were the first people to fly kites, about 2,300 years ago.

About 450 years ago Leonardo da Vinci designed an ornithopter (a machine with flapping wings) and a helicopter. But they never flew.

In 1783 a hot-air balloon built by the Montgolfier brothers of France carried aloft the first aviators.

The 1930s airship *Hindenburg* was the largest Zeppelin ever built. It was 800 feet long, three times longer than a Boeing 747 (230 feet).

Montgolfier balloon

Boeing 747

The first aviators to fly the Atlantic non-stop were Captain J. Alcock and Lieutenant A. W. Brown in a Vimy bomber, in 1919.

The first non-stop flight across the Pacific was in 1928, by the Americans Pangborn and Herndon.

The world's fastest airplane, the rocket-powered North American X-15, reached 4,534 mph in 1967.

Dick Rutan and Jeana Yeager in *Voyager* were first to fly around the world non-stop, without in-flight refueling, in 1986.

In 1927 Charles Lindbergh made the first solo flight across the Atlantic, in *Spirit of St. Louis*. The flight from New York to Paris took 33½ hours.

On December 17, 1903, at Kitty Hawk in North Carolina, Orville Wright became the first man to fly an airplane. The flight of 120 feet lasted under 12 seconds.

Wright Brothers' *Flyer*

86

Stealth bomber

Concorde

The top-secret U.S. Air Force Stealth bomber is the first warplane designed to be almost invisible to radar. It is probably the most expensive warplane of all time.

Concorde is the world's only supersonic airliner in service, carrying passengers since 1976. Only 16 Concordes were built by Britain and France.

·The first swing-wing jet was the U.S. F-111 bomber (1964). The idea of "variable geometry" or swing-wings was first thought of in the 1940s.

In 1947 the Bell XS-1 became the first aircraft to fly faster than sound in level flight.

swing-wing jet

Bell XS-1

Zeppelin

D-LZ12

HINDENBURG

glider

helicopter

Modern gliders can fly as far as 870 miles and as high as 49,000 feet using only air currents.

An experimental helicopter was tested in 1907. In 1936 Germany built the FW-61 (with two rotors), and in 1939 Igor Sikorsky's VS-300 was the forerunner of the modern single rotor helicopter.

Harrier

The first warplane able to take off and land vertically was Britain's Harrier "jump jet," which entered service in 1969.

INDEX

Note: page numbers in *italics* refer to illustrations

A

acupuncture·76, *76*
Africa 27, 29, 30, 31, 36, 41, 42, 45, 52, 56; exploration of 68, 69
African wild fig (tree) 34
aircraft 65, *65*, 78, 79, 86–7
airlines 79
airports 79
airships 86, *86*
Akbar, Emperor of India 66, *66*
albatrosses 41, *41*
Alcock and Brown (Captain J. *and* Lieut. A. W.) 86
Aldrin, Edwin 17
Alexander the Great 66, *66*
Alfred the Great 66, *66*
algae 35, *35*
algebra 62
Amazon rain forest 26, 30
Amburgh, Isaac Van 50
America (Central) 59
America (North) 26, 28, 65, *65*, 69, *see also* Canada; U.S.A.
America (South) 26, 27, 30, 33, 36, 37, 39, 40, 44, 56
American football 49, *49*
amphibians 32
Amundsen, Roald 69, *69*
anaconda, South American (snake) 36, *36*
anesthetics 77
anatomy 76, 77
Andes 24, 56, *56*
Andromeda Galaxy 12
Angel Falls (Venezuela) 23, *23*
angiosperms (plant family) 34
animals 36, 39, 40
Antarctic *see* polar regions
antelopes 31, *31*
Apollo space missions 17
Appert, Nicolas 44
Arabia, Ancient 62, *62*, 68
archaeology 60–1
Archaeopteryx 41, *41*
archer fish 39
Arctic *see* polar regions
Arctic terns 41, *41*

armor 65, *65*
Armstrong, Neil 17
artificial limbs 77
arts, the 46–7
Asia, Southeast 34, 45
asteroids 15
astronauts 17–19, *17–19*
Atacama (desert) 27
Atlantic Ocean 22, 56
atmosphere, Earth's 20, *20*, 28
atoms 70, *70*, 71, 74, *74*
Aurora Borealis 57, *57*
Australia 24, 33, 47, 51, 57, 58, 69
Australian sea wasp (jellyfish) 38
Ayers Rock (Australia) 57, *57*
Aztec pyramids 59, *59*

B

Bach, J. S. *47*
bacteria 71
Baird, John Logie 50
ballet 46
balloons 86, *86*
Baluchitherium (prehistoric mammal) 32, *32*
bamboo 35, *35*
Bangladesh 22, 79
Bannister, Roger 48
Barnard, Christiaan 77
barracudas (fish) *39*
baseball 48
bats (mammals) 40, *40*
batteries (electricity) 72
battles 17, 64–5
battleships 84
Beamon, Bob 48
bears 37
Beatles 51, *51*
Beaufort Scale (windspeed) 28
Becker, Boris 49
bees 40
beetles 36, *36*
Bell, Alexander Graham 73
Bell XS-1 (aircraft) 87, *87*
Benz, Karl 80
Bible, The 46
bicycles 79, 80
Big Bang theory 12, *12*
Big Boy (locomotive) 82, *82*
Big Muskie (earthmover) 81
birds 40–1
bird's nest soup 45

Birdseye, Clarence 72, *72*
Bismarck, Otto von 67, *67*
black dwarfs (stars) 13
black holes (stars) 13, *13*
blood 42, 43, 77
blue giants (stars) 13
blue whales 38, *38–9*
Bly, Nellie 78
body, human 42–3
Boeing 747 (airliner) 86, *86*
Bolivia 54, 85
bones, human 42, *42*
Booth, Hubert 73, *73*
Boudicca (Boadicea) 66, *66*
Brahms, Johannes *47*
Bramah, Joseph 72
Bras d'Or (hydrofoil) 85
Brazil 49, 52
Brazilian duckweed (wolfia) 35, *35*
bridges 58
Bullet Trains (Japan) 83
butterflies 40

C

Caesar, Gaius Julius 66, *66*
can-openers 73
Canada 22, 68, *see also* America (North)
canals 79
car racing 81
carriages (road) 81, *81*
Carter, Howard 60
Cartier, Jacques 68, *68*
castles 55, 58
catamarans 85, *85*
"cat's eyes" (road markets) 81
caves 25, *25*, 46
cells, body 42
Chain, Ernest 77
chalk cliffs 23, *23*
Channel Tunnel 83, *83*
Charlemagne 66, *66*
Charlotte Dundas (steamship) 85
cheetahs 36, *36*
Cheng-Ho (junk) 85
Chicago 59
Chile 27
China 24, 51, 53, 67, 68, 79; Ancient 28, 47, 58, 60, 62, *62–3*, 72, 73, 76, 86
chocolate 45
churches 58